I0094384

Accounting and Book-keeping for the Small Building Contractor

by Derek Miles

Intermediate Technology Publications

Published by ITDG Publishing
The Schumacher Centre for Technology and Development
Bourton Hall, Bourton-on-Dunsmore, Rugby, Warwickshire CV23 9QZ, UK
www.itdgpublishing.org.uk

First published in 1978
Reprinted 1986, 1993
Print on demand since 2004

ISBN 0 903031 54 X

A catalogue record for this book is available from the British Library

ITDG Publishing is the publishing arm of the Intermediate Technology
Development Group. Our mission is to build the skills and capacity of people
in developing countries through the dissemination of information
in all forms, enabling them to improve the quality of their lives and
that of future generations.

Printed in Great Britain by Lightning Source, Milton Keynes

Contents

Acknowledgements

The material upon which this volume is based was prepared for an I.L.O. African Regional Construction Management Course sponsored by N.O.R.A.D. (the Norwegian Aid Agency). The Intermediate Technology Development Group gratefully acknowledges their permission to publish, as well as the assistance of the Ministry of Overseas Development in financing earlier work in this field and the publication of this book.

Introduction

Management is about getting things done. Construction management is about getting things built. This book is the result of a decade of experience in helping small contractors in developing countries to get themselves established and to run their businesses effectively. The material has been used as a basis for training courses and should be invaluable for the managers and owners of small contracting businesses interested in improving their managerial capacity. This should in turn help them to become better employers, by offering more permanent jobs, as well as helping their clients by making the contractors more responsive to the needs of their customers.

As designs, materials and components have become more complex and demand has risen, the construction industry has taken on a key role and its performance impinges on all other sectors of the national economy. Thus construction costs are not merely a matter of concern to the clients of the industry, but must also concern the nation and its government. Indeed, construction is often responsible for creating more than half a nation's wealth in terms of fixed assets, so value for money must be a prime concern.

Speed of construction, as well as cost, is important. Unfortunately, local construction industries are often criticised by economists and others for failure to meet completion dates and, unfortunately, these criticisms are often justified due to inadequate performance. Indeed there is a vital link between time and money in construction management, and contractors usually find that quicker jobs lead to lower costs and bigger profits.

But governments and international aid agencies have a role in helping their local construction industry to become more competitive. One of the earliest efforts in this field was an Intermediate Technology Development Group project for 'Technological and procedural guidance to the construction industries of less-developed countries'. This was financed for the initial period (1969-72) by the British Ministry of

Overseas Development. During this period ITDG co-operated on the development of training material with the Kenya National Construction Corporation Ltd, which was started as a joint venture by the Kenya government and NORAD (the Norwegian Aid Agency) in 1967.

More recently the International Labour Office, with financial support from NORAD, has set up a project to promote the training of practical construction management within the African region. The immediate object was defined as 'to create in the participating countries a basic capability for delivering management training to small scale building contractors', while the longer term objective is to improve the overall managerial and economic performance of the contractors.

The material on which this book is based has been developed over the period. The approach is decidedly practical, with emphasis on providing ideas and techniques which the reader can apply in a straightforward way to increase his knowledge of, and control over, his business. Most of these ideas and techniques are just as relevant to good management in the public sector direct works agency as to running a private business for profit. Saving time — and saving money — are the twin themes.

No book of this kind can come from the innate knowledge of one individual alone. The author willingly acknowledges that he has drawn on ideas and experience from many people and many sources over the years. I would, however, like to mention four people with whom I have had the pleasure of talking and working as co-lecturer, on a number of occasions and in a number of countries. They are Dr Colin Guthrie and Mr John Andrews of the International Labour Organisation and Mr Folkward Vevstad and Mr Jostein Fjellestad, consultants to NORAD. Errors and omissions are, of course, my own. Finally, my thanks to the editorial staff of Intermediate Technology Publications Ltd for their care and effort in preparation.

Derek Miles

Chapter One

The Building Contract as a Financial Transaction

Importance of the construction industry in national development. Need to upgrade local industry. Intermediate building businesses. Risks of contracting. The building transaction. Management skills. Crucial role of financial management and estimating.

High risk

The construction industry is so complex that a high degree of skill and technical competence is required of businessmen who are engaged in it. The dangers facing the unskilled (or even just unlucky!) operators are shown by the fact that in one country after another building contractors head the list for bankruptcies, and limited companies trading in this area have a high risk of going into liquidation if their contracts prove unprofitable.

Financial control in public sector

Even in countries where all construction work is carried out within the public sector, there is the danger that poor management and a lack of appreciation of the importance of financial controls can result in a failure to achieve financial and physical production targets so that actual costs are in excess of budgetary allocation. Thus where we discuss the competitiveness and need for practical financial controls this should be of just as much interest to those who are responsible for the execution of work with public money in the public sector as to those who invest their private resources in the expectation of a satisfactory financial return.

Stability and strength

The aim, both for government and for the industry itself, should be to increase the stability and strength of the firms within it, because building and civil engineering operations are often the first requirement on the road to capital investment and an improved standard of living.

The need for building

In every country it is easy for any informed citizen to pick out the economic sectors which provide facilities which directly benefit the people and enable them to live a better life. I will mention some obvious examples. In the field of education most governments are committed to raising standards and increasing availability in their countries. So they must commission more schools, more technical and teacher training colleges. To improve the health of the population, more hospitals and clinics are needed. In many countries better transport facilities are a key to industrial and commercial development, so roads are also a very large item in the capital budget. Factories must be built, so that more goods can be made locally and people can be given more jobs. Literally, each and every area of development within a country requires the services of builders and it is vital that they should have sufficient knowledge and experience to play a full part in national development.

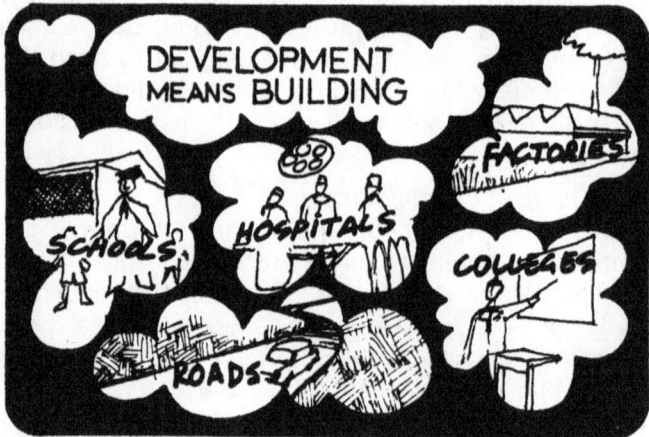

Capital expenditure

In fact, in most countries the construction industry itself absorbs between a half and two-thirds of the funds available for all capital investment each year, so the potential impact of better standards of efficiency in its building industry on a nation's economic performance is obvious. It is as a result of spending on capital expenditure that a country can expect to achieve a lasting return in the form of increased production of goods or better standards of services. It is a form of investment in the future, as the roads, dams, buildings and heavy machinery which it represents will go on yielding benefits for many years. It is the same with individuals and their business or personal budgets. When people spend money on capital goods — such as washing machines, radios, cars or new houses, they expect to get a return on that investment in terms of the services they will be able to enjoy as a result of the articles they have purchased.

Continuing benefit

Thus capital expenditure yields a continuing benefit over the years until the article or item is worn out and has to be replaced. It is also true to say that washing machines, like roads, will need to be maintained regularly until they have to be replaced. Just as it is foolish to buy an expensive motor car and then be too mean to keep it in good order by regular servicing and maintenance, it is also foolish for a client to commission an expensive building and then fail to keep it properly maintained. Therefore the competent builder should be ready to carry out maintenance work on existing buildings as well as to construct new works.

Importance of construction in developing countries

The share of construction in capital investment is important everywhere, and it has been estimated that throughout the world at least 50% of capital investment is spent on building and construction. Thus in all countries the construction industry is an important one, but in developing countries it is in a rather special position. This is because the existing

50%

OF CAPITAL INVESTMENT IS SPENT ON BUILDING AND CONSTRUCTION

stock of buildings and construction works is relatively low per head of population. There are proportionately fewer schools, hospitals and houses already built. Education, health and social welfare programmes are all held back if the buildings which they require are not available.

Crucial role

This lack of existing buildings and facilities means that the construction industry in a developing country has an especially crucial role. It must supply the country with a very large stock of buildings and civil engineering works to allow the government to catch up and provide its people with the services necessary to meet their economic and social development plans.

Growing demand

This means that there will be a tremendous amount of building and construction to be done in these countries in the foreseeable future. But the government and the people do not want to wait 20 or 30 years for these projects. It wants them as soon as possible. So the construction industry will have to meet this demand very soon. As the expenditure on capital investment increases so will the demand for the services of construction enterprises.

Private Clients

It is not only public sector building programmes that are likely to increase. In many countries, private clients will also commission an increasing volume of work from local builders. Individuals will need houses and estate developers will start private housing estates for sale or rent in addition to government financed housing programmes. Privately-owned factories and warehouses will be required in increasing numbers, and new offices, shops and commercial developments will be called for in large and small towns.

Increasing complexity of work

So there can be little doubt that competent contractors can be assured of an increasing amount of work to do in the years to come. But not only will there be more work in terms of volume. There is also a pattern of development which suggests that the buildings to be constructed, the types of construction and the method to be employed will become steadily more complex.

Meeting demands

The rising demand for University buildings and scientific laboratories implies a need for more complex structures than single-storey primary schools. The trend towards more complex building construction requiring more advanced technology has already begun. A walk through the centre of most capital cities provides a living proof of this. Even though they may doubt the wisdom of applying over-complicated technologies, contractors must be ready to meet the demands made upon them.

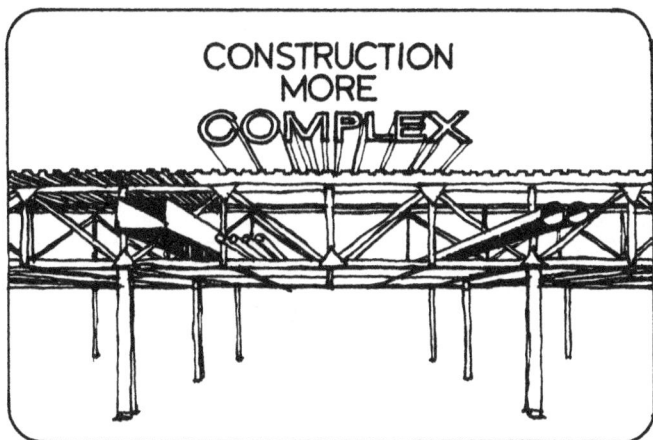

CONSTRUCTION
MORE
COMPLEX

Improving efficiency

Thus the construction industry is an important one, and most governments would be wise to consider every possible measure to improve its efficiency and performance. However, partly due to the very specialised technical and organisational skills it requires and partly due to the diversity of structures needed and the variety of contractors and public construction teams involved, it is an industry which can be changed only slowly.

Improvement takes time

Although training and re-organisation can sometimes yield quick dividends, it is more usual for the associated expenditure of time, money and effort to take rather longer to pay for itself, and it may take five to 10 years before a government sees a really significant impact in clear and measurable increased efficiency. Success depends on each individual construction enterprise analysing its own strengths and weaknesses and then, by taking steps to improve plotting and following a path to development. By this means, over a period of time, it is possible to acquire the skills, staff and equipment to become a modern 'professional' builder.

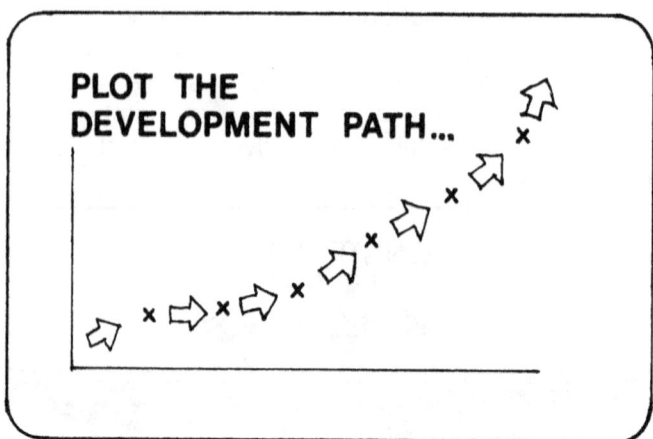

PLOT THE DEVELOPMENT PATH...

Slow to respond

In some countries the fact that the construction industry is slow to respond to development initiatives is taken as an excuse for doing nothing about it, on the grounds that the problems are here and now and that there is no time to worry about the medium and longer term. Although doing nothing is always easier and more tempting than taking a positive initiative, it is not always the wisest course of action. The result of doing nothing is that, over the years, these countries continue to be at the mercy of a high cost industry of limited efficiency, often dependent on expensive foreign resources and skills, and with no realistic hope of a change for the better. In short, for a government to ignore its construction industry and its needs is an act of passive sabotage which is bound to result in the nation failing to improve its capital resources and productive strength at the rate which it needs and which would otherwise be possible.

In most countries building programmes are still on the increase, and this means that more and more is demanded of local construction industries. Whether the work is done by public sector building teams, self help groups or private contractors, the work has to be done.

Who is to do the work and what training do they need?

Technical and business knowledge

The first requirement must be sufficient technical knowledge to understand the drawings, the materials and components that are to be used and the way in which they should be assembled. However it is equally important that a contractor should be a good businessman, which means that he should have the ability to plan and control his activities. Thus technical and business knowledge must be combined if a contractor is to put himself in a position to survive and progress.

THE
CONTRACTOR
NEEDS

TECHNICAL
KNOWLEDGE

BUSINESS
SKILLS

Organisations vary

The organisation of contracting firms varies enormously. At one end of the scale is the small jobbing business, consisting of perhaps one or two men, which carries out minor repairs, painting or plumbing. At the other end of the scale is the large international contractor carrying out multi-million dollar contracts all over the world. In between lie the many medium-sized businesses which individually carry out a handful of small or medium-sized jobs each year but which collectively are responsible for a very high proportion of every nation's building and civil engineering work.

Intermediate businesses

It is these medium-sized businesses each employing up to a hundred or so men, which are in some ways the most difficult to manage. The very small business is easy to manage because it is so small and the large contracting firm has sufficient financial resources to employ specialists and highly qualified professionals. But in these medium-sized or 'intermediate' businesses the owner or his manager must know enough about all the many specialised functions to control them all himself, so that his business can be planned and operated in a systematic way.

Two routes

There are two routes to becoming a contractor. The first is upwards through the industry, starting by learning a craft, then going on to become a foreman with an established contractor or possibly a clerk-of-works or site supervisor, and finally building up enough savings, experience and confidence to start out on one's own. The other route is to move across into construction from some other form of commercial undertaking, such as retailing or manufacturing, and apply this commercial experience to the activity of building.

Easy to underestimate difficulties

In both categories there are many new contractors who underestimate the difficulties of the business activity that they have chosen to undertake. At first sight a building business may seem an almost foolproof way to make money. It appears that all the businessman has to do is to obtain a contract, then buy materials from the cheapest source, recruit a gang of experienced men and ensure that they assemble the materials as shown on the drawings that the architect or engineer will provide. Where materials can be purchased on credit, it may be possible to delay payment until interim payments have been received from the client so that a contract can be largely self-financing. Added to these apparently favourable factors is the powerful attraction of those businessmen who have prospered in the industry, since the corollary of high risk is high potential and an operator with high ability and good luck can prosper very rapidly indeed.

Taking risks

What these optimists tend to overlook is the fact that a building contractor is effectively not just selling his technical skill; he is also selling insurance. If the client was to undertake the work with his own directly-recruited workforce he would have to pay directly for any unexpected costs. If the ground conditions were difficult or materials deliveries were delayed or his employees failed to carry out the work properly, he would pay directly for the costs resulting from these contingencies. The advantage to the client of putting the work out to contract is that it removes the worry of building from him and transfers it to the shoulders of the contractor.

THE CONTRACTOR SELLS 'INSURANCE'.

AND TAKES RISK OF INCREASED COSTS

CLIENT

Risks transferred

Once he has accepted the lowest or best tender for the work, providing that his chosen contractor has sufficient experience and working capital, he is relieved of risk and knows what he will have to pay. But building is a risky business and risks do not disappear. The risks are transferred to the contractor, who hopes that with planning, skill and good organisation his actual costs will be sufficiently lower than the tender figure to yield an acceptable profit.

All right on the site?

It is in the nature of most human beings to underestimate risks, and potential contractors are among the most optimistic of men. Just as actors comfort themselves with the belief that their performance will be 'all right on the night', so a contractor believes that his activities will be 'all right on the site'. But in addition to the hoped-for prospect of easy money, a further attraction is that building contracting is not a particularly difficult business to enter.

Easy to register

In many countries it is relatively easy to register as a contractor for small building contracts, as little evidence of technical competence or business ability is demanded. Once he has registered, the potential contractor is free to tender for any contract which becomes available within the category for which he has registered.

Shortage of working capital

If he is fortunate enough to be awarded a contract, he will probably hire labour on a temporary basis for the duration of the job, borrow a small concrete mixer and other basic equipment and try to obtain materials shortly before they are to be used. In this way he will cut his need for working capital to a minimum, although this strategy may well lead to a sacrifice of speed and quality of construction as well as potential profit. It is likely that he will attempt to juggle his finances through from one interim payment to the next, often delaying wage payments and settlement of suppliers' accounts in order to achieve even this.

Occasional contractors

Eventually the job is completed and, if it shows a profit, he will be encouraged to take his turn in the queue once again for future work. He may even have ended the contract with a few small tools or items of plant, which can be stored

THE OCCASIONAL CONTRACTOR

for future use. He will have joined the ranks of the occasional contractors, who are not sufficiently committed to dedicate

16

themselves to study and gain experience in the industry but contribute to the severe competition for small contracts which makes life so difficult for those contractors who have a more serious and long term approach. Indeed these 'occasional contractors' survive during and between contracts by applying strategies and techniques which would increase the likelihood of failure on larger jobs.

The building transaction

Before we go on to discuss what a contractor needs to know, we should find out a little more about him and the nature of the problems which he faces. A start might be made by examining the nature of the transaction with which a building contractor is involved and comparing it with the sort of transaction which is experienced by other businessmen such as shopkeepers, manufacturers or wholesalers.

Time span of typical contract

A typical small to medium-sized building contract may take six months to execute, and will be followed by a six month maintenance period (at least) while the contractor waits for the release of the remainder of his retention money. To gauge the overall time span of the transaction we can assume that, in a typical case, a fixed price tender will have been prepared and submitted to the client's professional advisers some two or three months before work is started on the site.

Long period of uncertainty

It is true that interim payments will be received as the work proceeds, but the fact remains that the eventual success or failure of each individual transaction (in terms of profit or loss) cannot be accurately determined until 15-18 months after the original offer and commitment. This lengthy period of financial uncertainty would be bad enough in itself, but in addition each individual transaction involves a substantial sum of money, often as much as a quarter or even a third of the firm's total annual turnover.

Looking ahead

Thus even the small building contractor has to look a long way ahead compared to his neighbours who own shops or run other small businesses.

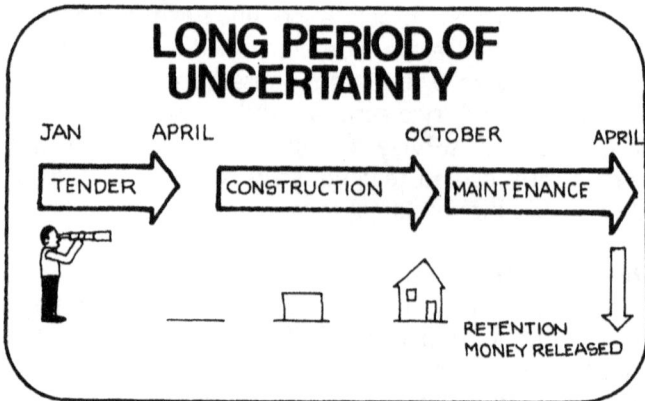

LONG PERIOD OF UNCERTAINTY

JAN — APRIL — OCTOBER — APRIL

TENDER → CONSTRUCTION → MAINTENANCE →

RETENTION MONEY RELEASED

Practices, problems and needs

Despite the importance of the construction industry as the spearhead of national development, surprisingly little effort has gone into studying the difficulties facing small- and intermediate-sized businesses in this vital industrial sector. One of the few systematic studies of African building enterprises was carried out by the Intermediate Technology Development Group Ltd. in Kenya. This study of the case histories of indigenous Kenyan contractors was entitled *Kenyan Building Contractors: Practices, Problems and Needs.* *

Management Skills

It suggested that basic management rather than advanced technical skills is the key to survival in this competitive business. There is no reason to suppose that these problems are peculiar to Kenya, and much evidence to suggest that it is a general (and understandable) weakness in this industrial sector. Many practitioners lack basic relevant skills and only those who overcome this lack are most likely to prosper. One quotation is particularly relevant:

'The common factor in the case histories of these four successful one-man firms seems to be the stress laid by the principals on shrewd financial planning and control. This does not usually imply a particularly sophisticated system of documentation, and the firm's 'filing system' often depends mainly on the memory of the proprietor. This is

*Obtainable from Intermediate Technology Publications Ltd., 9 King Street, London WC2E 8HN, U.K.

a potential weakness that can be expected to show up more clearly as the businesses expand to a stage where additional managers have to be brought in.'

Lack of funds?

Although working capital is always a problem for building contractors and most comment that it is a lack of funds which really holds them back, the truth is usually a little more complex. First one should ask why the funds are not available. It is not due merely to prejudice on the part of potential lenders. In fact many lenders would say that the reason why they are so reluctant to lend or give credit to builders is the result of hard experience. The truth is more likely that it is the lack of knowledge and experience in the proper control of money which makes a builder so vulnerable, and good financial control could reduce his risks to a great extent and make him more credit-worthy.

WHY WON'T PEOPLE LEND TO BUILDING CONTRACTORS ?

Concentrate on finance

Thus this series will concentrate on the financial side of the building business. For, if a contractor keeps accurate books and accounts, if he is able to produce realistic estimates and tenders and if he can effectively plan his finances and cash flow, he should stand a much better chance of survival and steady progress.

The tender

The first stage in the financial transaction that every contract represents is the submission of a tender based on a specification, drawings and other information provided by the architect or engineer who has been appointed by the client as his technical adviser or representative. This tender should be based on an estimate of what the contractor will have to pay out in order to cover his costs on the contract. He will then add a percentage to this figure to provide a profit which should represent a reasonable return on the money invested in the business, bearing in mind the contractual risks associated with the particular job which is being tendered for.

Tests judgement

It is at this first stage that the would-be contractor is faced with his first problem and his judgement is tested for the first time. For he will be tendering in the hope of obtaining work, but whether the job is in fact awarded to him depends not only on his own tender but on those of other contractors who have to make up their own minds as to the costs of carrying out the work and the level of profit which they will seek.

Accurate estimating

Thus, even if the tender is based on an accurate estimate of the costs of carrying out the job in an efficient manner and the percentage added for profit is reasonable, the contractor may still fail to get the job. However, if the job is bound to result in a loss it is best to leave it to competitors and concentrate on attracting an order book of work that is at least potentially profitable. The contractor who has the ability and experience to produce estimates and tenders that reliably reflect the costs and risks that are likely to be involved gives himself the best chance of survival in the longer term.

The operational phase

Once he has heard that his was the lowest acceptable tender and that he has been awarded the contract, the contractor can turn his attention to the operational phase. He must ensure that the work is properly carried out according to the drawings and specification and that it is completed within the allotted contract period. He will need to plan the work so that it is profitable and that the cash flow on the contract is such that working capital is within agreed limits for borrowing.

Control

Right through this operational phase until the contract has been handed over to the client, the contractor needs to be aware of his financial position and to know whether costs and receipts are in accordance with his original plan. It is important to have figures available promptly, even if they are only approximate, so that remedial action can be taken whenever necessary, and his aim should be to have a good general understanding of financial techniques.

Aim of the book

The intention of the remaining chapters in this book is to introduce the contractor to the basic principles of book-keeping and accounting, so that he can better understand his business. Building will always be a high risk business but, by efficient financial management, it is possible to quantify the risks and take quick action when things start to go wrong.

Application

It will be for the individual reader to consider and decide the way in which the techniques can best be applied to his own business. But the book will be a failure if they are not applied, since the success or failure of a contracting business is judged in practice rather than theory. Our target is not just learning for learning's sake. It is to enable private sector enterprises to cut costs so that they can get more contracts and gain more profit. It is for public sector organisations to do a better job for the people that they serve.

Chapter Two

Organising The Office: Documentation

Book-keeping and bankruptcy. Documentation: the key to financial control. Form design. Contract variation forms. Measuring extra works. Job sheets. Daily labour allocation sheets. Labour analysis and costing. Purchase orders. Materials sheets. Plant and transport records. Banking records. Petty cash transactions.

Book-keeping and bankruptcy

Book-keeping and paperwork is certainly not the most exciting part of running a building business. Most contractors are practical men and are happiest and feel most comfortable when they are on one of their building sites giving instructions to their foremen and generally directing operations. For many of them book-keeping just gives them headaches and takes up valuable time. Poor written records are a feature of too many small businesses — just as in a high proportion of bankruptcies. In fact there is probably some connection, because very few businessmen go bankrupt as a result of spending too much time keeping their books up to date but very many find their way to the bankruptcy court without any written evidence of their sales, purchases and commitments.

Too few hours in the day

This is not to suggest that small contractors are very different from other small businessmen, all of whom tend to find that there are just too few hours in the day to allow them to keep their paperwork up to date. However, while written records of some kind are important in any kind of business, for the builder they are vital.

Need for accurate information

The contractor usually has to stand by the unit prices which he has estimated and included in a fixed price tender, prepared well in advance of starting work on the site, whatever difficulties and unforeseen problems he might encounter. During the course of the contract he has to make large payments for labour, materials and plant well in advance of receiving payments from his client. We discussed the long time lag between the start and finish of the construction transaction in the previous chapter, and this is another reason why the building contractor is in particular need of up to date and accurate information.

Guide and control

The object of this chapter is to outline the minimum records that must be kept if the contractor is to be able to *guide* and *control* his business rather than just be carried along by it. But guidance and control is just not possible without accurate information. The reason for concentrating on providing accurate information is thus to allow the manager to manage his business effectively, and good information in the end results in good profits.

Guide to Records and Control

The nerve centre

The manager in his office represents the nerve centre of a contracting firm. From the office, instructions are sent to site foremen, decisions are made as to which items of plant to buy and where it is to be deployed, which contracts are to be tendered for and at which price. In addition, progress reports from the sites are studied, and where they show slow progress or unexpected costs, they are investigated.

Fitness

Thus the head office is the brain of the organisation and, as with the human brain, if it fails to work properly and efficiently, disaster will result. For it is just as true in business life as in nature that only the fit survive in the long run. So fitness in this sense must be the first objective of the serious businessman. To be fit in business is to be a good manager.

Good management

A manager is judged as good or bad not by his academic qualifications, but by the quality of his practical decisions. Thus good management consists above all in putting oneself in the best possible position to make good decisions quickly as soon as a problem has been identified or brought to the attention of the manager. Some businessmen think that they know their businesses so well that they have all the possible knowledge that could be required about it in their heads. But what happens as they get older or their businesses get bigger? There must come a time when even these businessmen begin to forget important items, and their operations suffer as a direct result. What is more, if they have no system of making, keeping and using written records, it will take a long time to get things back under control.

Documentation

Thus even the small businessman, if he is ambitious, should keep appropriate written records of his transactions with all the documents neatly and tidily filed in his office. As he starts out, his office may just be one room, but it still makes sense to see that all necessary records and information are kept readily available.

Rely on staff

As his business grows, the contractor will have to rely more and more on information gathered by his staff rather than himself personally, and it will be necessary to train them to present written information clearly.

Site records

Thus he should encourage the foreman on the building site to use a simple job programme to see whether he is behind schedule or not. A clear record of materials delivered, used and on site is needed.

Key to financial control

Good documentation is a key to proper financial control and accurate forecasts of profit and cash flow. It is also necessary to document transactions so that good credit control can be achieved, to check that clients are not failing to honour certificates and are paying their debts promptly. Just as the house that the contractor is to build must be provided with a good foundation, so the basic business needs of a contracting business cannot be met without a foundation of good *documentation.*

Planning documentation

As with other business activities, good documentation does not just 'happen'. It has to be thought about and planned by the contractor to suit his own special needs.

Four resources

Just as a sensible builder will plan his work, so he should plan his system of documentation to fit in with his needs as a manager of resources. The four resources which he has at his command are:

Men
Materials
Plant and tools
Money

The way in which all these resources are used will determine whether or not his business is efficient and profitable, and the use of each will have to be documented and checked regularly to ensure that no wastage occurs.

Information costs money

It is not suggested that any kind of information about a contractor's business must be of use to him. Information, like everything else the contractor needs to carry on his business, costs money and there is no point in gathering data unless it is in a suitable form for practical use in managing the business and keeping a record of its financial performance.

Readable and accessible

If they are to be of any real value to a businessman, the record books and other documents must be both readable and accessible. Too often the site records of a small contracting firm are scribbled on any odd piece of paper that comes to hand, such as the back of an old envelope. Then when the owner visits the site the foreman goes through his pockets to see what he can find (although some will by now have been lost). When the owner gets back to his office, he again turns out his pockets and those records which have not been lost on the way are dumped in an untidy pile on his desk. All this muddle occurs because the contractor 'cannot find the time for paperwork and filing', but the truth is that he wastes three or four times as much time when he comes to search for delivery notes to check a supplier's account or the records needed to submit an interim or final account. These last few sentences may seem to be just a cartoon of how any reasonable contractor would behave, but unfortunately far too many contractors fail to keep their records in a usable form, so that they are both *readable* and *accessible.*

Books and standard forms

The best way to make sure that records are kept in a readable and accessible way is to make use of books and standard forms. If financial transactions are regularly written up in large hard-covered books then there will be no reason to fear that individual sheets may be lost. Other records, such as time sheets, which are required regularly but which could not conveniently be kept in a book, are best kept on standard duplicated forms. In some cases it may be possible to buy suitable standard forms from the local stationer's shop, but some parts of every business are special to itself and so special forms have to be thought up to suit these special purposes.

Forms should be easy to use

Although the cost of duplicating or printing forms can be quite heavy, they may still be worthwhile if they save a large amount of time for the contractor and his employees as well as keeping records in a condition that allows them to be referred to and used whenever they are needed. The important thing is to check that forms are properly designed so that they are easy to use, and there is just enough space to fill in the information that is really needed to run the business effectively and keep proper records.

Design of forms

Form design is a matter for responsible management, not something to be left to the clerk or site foreman. Once a form is in use, it will have to be filled in regularly by a large number of employees and used by many others. They will do this in the contractor's time, not in their own, so careful thought needs to be given to ensure that they have no need to waste time writing down facts and figures that will never be used. When the form has been designed it should be discussed with the employees who will have to use it, as they may be able to make some useful suggestions on possible improvements.

FORM DESIGN

1 THINK IT OUT CAREFULLY.

2 DISCUSS WITH EMPLOYEES WHO WILL USE IT.

Some rules

Some good rules to follow when designing a form are:

1. Use a standard paper size.
2. Use the smallest possible size which will give enough detail.
3. Make sure quality of paper is sufficient to stand up to rough use on site, and that it will take ink, pencil or ball point pens.
4. Leave a margin on left hand side for filing (and pre-punch holes if necessary).
5. Don't waste space in unnecessary headings.
6. Where figures are to be added (e.g. time sheet) design form so that they will be listed in a vertical column.

7. Printed alternatives for ticking or deleting may save writing time (and therefore costs!).
8. If possible arrange the form so that it does more than one job (e.g. by adding columns to a time sheet so that the clerk can calculate bonus payments).
9. Carefully check the wording and instructions of the form (and try it out on employees who will have to use it) to make sure it is quite clear.
10. Give clear instructions to the printer and attach a reference number for re-ordering.

Regular review

Although a documentation system can start off as an efficient operation providing the right information at the right time, this can change as the business grows and itself changes. Thus it is wise to take a fresh look at the system occasionally to ensure that all the information that is gathered is useful and to see if there is any way in which it could be gathered more efficiently. This regular review might well take place once a year as the businessman prepares his annual accounts.

Some forms needed by all contractors

Although it would not be sensible to try to lay down a set of forms that would be needed by all contractors everywhere, there are some which are generally required to keep track of the major resources employed in the business and also of changes in the contract itself. The need for some will become clear as a result of experience but, just as information itself costs time and money to gather, the contractor must also remember that lack of information may itself be expensive. For example, the client through the architect might require additional work such as a deepening of foundations. If there is no written evidence available at the end of the contract, the final measurement will be based on the drawings and the contractor will lose money.

Contract variation forms

It is unusual for any building or civil engineering project to be constructed exactly in accordance with the drawings, bill of quantities and specification. The contract documents are usually prepared well in advance of the work, and the client may change his mind later about fittings, windows, doors or even room sizes. It is also difficult for any architect or engineer to be absolutely sure about soil types or future availability of proprietary materials or components. The changes in the work that result will cause changes, often increases, in cost for the contractor, which he will be entitled to recover from the contingency provision in his accepted tender. Each individual change will probably represent a fairly small sum, but altogether the full recovery of increased costs may make all the difference between profit and loss.

Extra works order

The basic contract variation form is called an **extra works order.** This simply records the amount of extra work that is required so that the cost can be calculated accurately after the job has been done, and must be signed by the architect or his clerk of works as an authorised variation in the contract.

Must be signed

The contractor should instruct his foremen never to carry out work which is additional to that described in the drawings and contract documents unless a proper works order has been signed. Even where a change occurs which will incur no extra cost (such as the substitution of one type of brick for another specified), authorisation should be obtained. The contractor originally tendered for the work on the basis of a specific-ation, contract drawings and bill and quantities and, unless changes are properly authorised on behalf of the client by his site representative, those documents remain the legal basis for the contract. If a clerk of works should be replaced during the course of a contract and changes have been made by the contractor on the basis of a verbal instruction or verbal agree-ment, not only may he fail to receive payment for the additional work but he may also be required to replace the altered work according to the original contract.

Value at end of contract

The value of a definite procedure for authorising extra work becomes clear at the end of the contract, when the contractor has to prepare and submit a final account. He can then collect together all the extra works orders for the contract and calculate the amount due on each of them in turn, without having to search through his memory to try to recall events that are long past. In this way he is able to ensure that he receives payment in full for all his additional work.

Items in extra works order

Contractors usually design forms to suit their own purposes, but the essential items to be included in an extra works order are as follows:

1. Job number or name of contract.
2. Date.
3. Description of extra work.
4. Contract work to be omitted (if any).
5. Method of carrying out the work (any particular plant to be used, etc.).
6. Method of measurement.
7. Space for signature by client's representative.

Job no......   **Date:**

Details of Extra Work:

Work to be Omitted:

Method:

Measurement:

Authorised by:
(For Client.)

AN EXTRA WORKS ORDER

30

Serial numbering

A useful safeguard to ensure that no works orders are accidentally lost and therefore forgotten is to number all the orders for each job from one onwards. After signature it is best to keep them all in a file so that it is easy to check through regularly and make sure that none are missing.

Copies

Works orders should always be in duplicate as the client's representative will require a copy in addition to the one to be kept by the contractor, and it may be better to have them in triplicate so that a copy can be sent to the contractor's head office in addition to the one to be kept on the site. Where there is a good reason to expect a large number of orders to be needed, it may be best to use a duplicate or triplicate bound book so that carbon copies of all orders are automatically bound together.

Methods of measurement

There are three main methods of measuring extra works:

1. Measured at contract rates.
2. Agreed fixed price.
3. Dayworks.

Measured at contract rates

Where the variation proposed is a comparatively small addition to similar work specified in the contract, such as an additional annexe to a building or an additional run of drainage, it is usually appropriate to agree to measure the extra work at the rates agreed in the contract. If this method is employed, a contractor who has priced his unit rates erratically might find himself in the position of being obliged to carry out the extra work at a loss. Most contracts permit the client's representative to vary quantities without re-negotiating rates unless a major change in the contract is proposed.

Check unit costs

The experienced contractor will think about this possibility at the tendering stage. New contractors sometimes think that all that matters is that the total tender figure should be below those of their competitors, but only just below so that they can make a good profit. They don't worry so much about the unit prices so long as the multiplication and addition leads to the correct tender figure. As they become more experienced they realise that getting the contract is only part of the battle for financial survival. The more important part is to ensure that it shows a profit. Thus, besides good planning and management, it is wise to look at the work to be carried out in a critical way and try to foresee which items in the bill may exceed the stated quantities.

Example

For example there may be a small provisional item for excavation in rock and the contractor with local knowledge might know that a lot of rock is likely to have to be excavated under a particular foundation. In this case he would make quite sure that his unit price for excavation in rock covered his costs and yielded a reasonable percentage profit, while a less knowledgeable competitor might price the item low and have to work at a loss if he was awarded the contract.

Agreed fixed price

Where the extra work is relatively small in value, the contractor may agree a fixed price with the client's representative. This has the advantage for the contractor that he will not usually be required to keep any particular records of the work, thereby saving on clerical work. However, it may be worthwhile to make a quick calculation of the cost involved for guidance in future negotiations.

Dayworks

The third method of measurement is known as dayworks, in which the contractor is directly reimbursed for the costs involved in carrying out the extra work with a percentage addition for profit. The costs of supplying labour, plant and equipment are calculated on the basis of specified hourly rates and the total value of work done with the associated materials cost (plus percentage profit) is calculated for each day. It is then signed by the client's representative, and is paid for with the next interim certificate.

Dayworks forms

If a great deal of dayworks is expected, it may be worth having special sheets printed or duplicated. Otherwise it is best to keep a special duplicate or (better) triplicate book for the purpose, so that there is less danger of any sheets being lost. Dayworks should show a guaranteed profit to the contractor, but the amount is small in percentage terms. Thus it is vital to ensure that no records are lost so that all costs will be fully covered.

Small jobs

Some of the work entrusted to local contractors is so small that a full contract is not justified, and it is carried out on a payments basis similar to that for extra work on a large contract.

Job sheet

For work of this kind a form called a 'job sheet' is useful, as illustrated below. This should give sufficient information to provide a proper invoice for the client after completion.

Typical Job Sheet

```
                         JOB   SHEET


        Job No.                   Address:


        Gang:          Foreman/Charge Hand        Date:



        Work Carried Out:






        Extra Work or Variations:







        Date started:
        Date finished:

        Additional Expenses:
```

Resource records

The other forms used by a contractor are mostly needed to keep track of the resources which he has to use to conduct his business. The four main resources which are involved are:

1. Labour
2. Materials
3. Plant and transport
4. Finance

Labour records

A record of the number of hours worked each day by all employees is essential in order to calculate wage payments, as well as for general costing purposes and as the basis for day-works calculations.

The time sheet

The basic labour record is the time sheet, which shows the number of hours worked by each man on a particular site and is usually filled in every day by the site foreman. In a jobbing business the time sheet might refer to a gang and show separately which jobs they worked on, but for contractors with larger individual contracts the more usual type of form is that shown below:

Job no..... Week ending:									
Name	Hours worked								total
	M	T	W	T	F	S	Sn		
1									
2									
3									
4									
5									
6									
total									

A TIME SHEET

Daily labour allocation sheet

Where more detail is required, a daily labour allocation sheet can be used. This gives a breakdown of the work carried out by each man on a particular site during the day, and can be divided to show the number of hours spent in excavation, concreting, etc. Although it means more work for the foreman in filling the sheet in each day, the sheets can yield very valuable information for costing purposes. An example is shown below:

Typical Daily Labour Allocation Sheet

DAILY LABOUR ALLOCATION

Job No.   Address:

Gang: Foreman/Charge Hand: Date:

TASK										TOTAL HOURS PER MAN
NAME	No.									
HOURS PER TASK										

Payroll calculations

At the end of each week the completed time sheets and/or labour allocation sheets should be sent to the head office as quickly as possible. Here it will be used immediately for payroll calculations. Gross wages are calculated by multiplying the number of hours worked by the hourly rate, possibly with an addition for overtime after a specified number of hours have been worked. It may be worthwhile adding a space on the time sheet for these calculations, so as to reduce the number of books and pieces of paper involved. Different countries have different regulations regarding statutory deductions from pay for taxes, etc. These additional calculations are carried out separately, and suitable printed forms and duplicate books are sometimes available locally.

Calculations must be accurate

Payroll calculations must be carried out quickly and accurately because employees rightly expect to be paid properly and on time. If wages are lower than they should be, even the more loyal employees will be annoyed and lose faith in the firm. If the miscalculation goes the other way and they are overpaid, they may not let the employer know and will in that event be faced with a smaller wage packet the following week. So, on grounds of industrial relations as well as financial control, these calculations must be carefully done.

Labour analysis and costing

Time sheets and payroll records will also be required for labour analysis and costing. Costing techniques will be discussed later, but the techniques cannot produce results unless the basic information is accurate. Thus records should be filed carefully so that it will be possible to charge wage payments either to the appropriate job or to general overheads.

Materials records

Materials are a major cost item in most contractor's businesses. Care must be taken to ensure that materials supplied are exactly in accordance with the specification, that goods are purchased at the most reasonable available prices, that stores are not lost, damaged or stolen and that costs are properly allocated. Good records are needed to help the contractor achieve all these ends.

Receipts

In the very small business nearly all goods are purchased for cash and, although this increases the need for working capital, it enables records and book-keeping to be kept very simple. All that the contractor needs to do is to ensure that he keeps his business transactions separate from private household purchases and that receipts are always issued by suppliers. Then he simply has to collect together the receipts regularly and enter them in a purchase book so that the costs can be allocated.

Credit accounts

Once a contractor has been trading satisfactorily for a few years, it is often possible to negotiate credit accounts with main suppliers. This has the useful effect of delaying payments, thereby improving cash flow and easing working capital requirements. But it also means that documentation systems and financial control must be made more stringent. It is easier to buy goods on credit than when cash has to be found immediately, but the invoices and statement will come in at the end of the month. These will have to be checked and the money found.

Two tasks

There are two tasks at that stage. Firstly, it is necessary to check that the account is correct and the goods have actually been supplied. Secondly, there must be accurate financial control to ensure that there is sufficient cash in hand and at the bank to pay the suppliers account promptly. It is the job of the documentation system to ensure that both of these functions can be properly fulfilled.

Purchase order

The first step in a credit transaction is the purchase order, issued by the contractor to the supplier and asking him to supply goods of a certain quality. It represents a miniature contract in itself (between the contractor and his supplier) and should state:
1. Name and address of supplier
2. Date
3. Quantity of order
4. Brief specification and description of quality

5. Unit price
6. Total price
7. Agreed discount (if any) and terms of payment (credit period).

Contractor X

TO: *(SUPPLIER)*

DATE:

Please supply:

(ITEM; QUANTITY, QUALITY, PRICE AND DISCOUNT.)

Signed:
(For Contractor X)

EXAMPLE OF A
PURCHASE ORDER

Effective communication

One good reason for using written purchase orders is that they ensure effective communication with the supplier, so that he will have no reason to misunderstand what is required. This is particularly important when certain materials or components have long delivery times, since mistakes in quantity or quality can lead to expensive hold-ups later on the site. Purchase orders are also most useful if available in duplicate or triplicate book form, so that one can be given to the supplier and a copy kept by the contractor.

Authorised signatures

The contractor must decide which of his employees should be authorised to sign purchase orders, and suppliers should be notified that only purchase orders bearing one of these signatures will be honoured. Purchase order books should be treated with the same care as cheque books since, if one was stolen, the thief might be able to obtain building materials and sell them, leaving the contractor with the responsibility for paying the supplier.

Delivery notes

When goods are delivered to the site, the supplier's driver will usually bring a delivery note and ask the site foreman to sign a copy to confirm that it has been delivered. Foremen should always be instructed to check all deliveries carefully, and amend the delivery note if any items are not as ordered or have been broken in transit. The contractor's copy of the delivery note should be sent to his office weekly with the time sheet.

Materials sheet

Once the materials have been delivered, the contractor will need to keep track of how they are used. This gets more difficult as the business expands with a central store being

Typical Materials Sheet

MATERIALS SHEET

Job No.   Address:

Gang: Foreman/Charge Hand: Date:

DESCRIPTION	MAKE	CATALOGUE NO.	SIZE	RECEIVED AT JOB		RETURNED TO STORE	
				QUANTITY	VALUE	QUANTITY	VALUE

established and more transfers take place between the growing number of sites. A form which will help with this is the materials sheet, illustrated below, showing for each site the materials received and returned to store.

Check stock levels

The materials sheet should be filled in weekly by the site foreman, and submitted with the copies of delivery notes (with which it should of course agree). It will be used to check on materials costs in relation to those forecast at the time of tendering. In addition it is wise to keep a check on stocks if a central store is used. Although bulk buying and distribution through a central store can reduce costs, high stocks can mean increased demands for working capital as well as the risk of pilferage and specialised items becoming obsolete.

Plant and transport

The small/medium sized contractor will probably not have a great deal of plant but, even so, its value will be quite large in relation to the overall value of his business. A contractor with good plant and equipment has a useful advantage in tackling the larger or more difficult jobs, but hourly and daily costs are large and some costs (depreciation etc) go on whether the plant is being used or not. So plant documentation should provide a basis for keeping the plant as fully occupied as possible, and for accurately allocating costs to individual sites, so that site foremen will not keep plant after it is really needed.

Keep costs separate

All plant and transport costs, other than those for small items of equipment and tools, should be kept separate. This will allow the contractor to judge objectively whether each item is earning its keep. It is surprising that some contractors who are harsh with their employees and expect them to work non-stop do not realise that their plant and transport is only working effectively for two or three hours a day. Plant documentation should yield sufficient information to judge when plant should be sold or replaced, and to make a fair comparison between labour-intensive and plant-intensive ways of getting the job done.

Vehicle log books

One basic source of information for vehicles is the log book, which should be filled in daily by the driver. Some of the items which should be shown in the log book are:

1. Work done on each job
2. Mileage covered
3. Petrol and oil purchased
4. Any damage or faults
5. Repairs or servicing.

Maintenance records

Where mechanical plant or vehicles are employed, regular maintenance must be carried out in accordance with the manufacturer's instructions. Thus it is important to set up some form of system to check regularly on which items are due for maintenance, as well as relying on drivers or operators for this information. In a small firm this can be a simple checklist showing speedometer readings or dates at which servicing is due, against which the manager can check when this must be done.

Plant costs

Although it is difficult to prescribe exactly which forms will have to be used by every contractor, it can be said that sufficient information must be gathered to calculate costs accurately under the following headings:

1. Drivers' or operators' wages
2. Fuel and oil
3. Servicing and maintenance
4. Major repairs
5. Taxation and licensing
6. Insurance
7. Depreciation (including adjustments for sale of plant).

Hired plant

Where plant can be hired at reasonable rates, this may be a cheaper answer than buying outright. Charges for hired plant must be kept separate from those for the builder's own plant, and the same principles apply as to controlling purchases of building materials. However, special care should be taken to see that the plant hire firm does not charge for a longer period than agreed, and that periods when the plant was broken down or being serviced are deducted.

Finance

Particular care must be taken with information relating to the builder's fourth resource — finance. He must devise an accounting and documentation system that will cover both cash and credit transactions, and enable the contractor to assess his assets and liabilities regularly to avoid any danger of insolvency.

Using a bank

Some small contractors think that their business is too small for it to be worthwhile to open a bank account. This is foolish, since it is the small contractor who is particularly in need of the advice and the documentation that a bank can provide.

Banking records

One disadvantage of cash transactions is that some payment advices or invoices can be lost, so that the record of the transactions can be incomplete leading to inaccurate accounts. This cannot happen if a bank account is employed, since it provides a ready-made documentation of payments and receipts. The cheque book stubs and paying in book give the user of a banking account a direct record of his transactions, and bank statements are provided regularly which can be of great assistance in checking accounts.

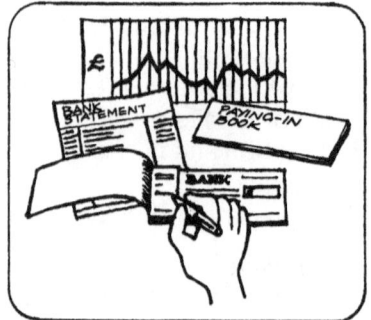

OPERATING A BANK ACCOUNT PROVIDES READYMADE DOCUMENTATION OF PAYMENTS AND RECEIPTS

Keep your own records

Although a bank account can be a great help in providing and confirming financial information in a readable form, even banks can occasionally make clerical errors and bank statements should be carefully checked. Also the contractor should keep a record of payments and receipts between statements to ensure that his account never runs into deficit or over agreed overdraft limits.

42

Bank charges

Most banks make a charge for operating a current account, although no charge may be made if the account is kept well in credit. However, these charges are usually quite low compared to the cost of employing a clerk to keep track of a lot of cash payments. In addition the bank manager can provide very valuable financial advice to the inexperienced businessman.

Cash transactions

No businessman can get by without some cash transactions. To start with, most employees will want to be paid in cash.

Wage payments

It is usually best to calculate the total sum due in wages each week and draw the exact amount of the bank with an open cheque. This has the advantage that the contractor can calculate exactly how much small change he will require to make up each wage packet to the right amount and draw the right coinage and denomination of notes from the bank. Where possible, it is best to get employees to sign for their wage packets so that there is no danger of argument at a later date.

Cash receipts

Builders who work for the private sector may be paid in cash by their clients, but this cash can immediately be paid into the builder's bank account and a note of the name of the payee can be made on the counterfoil of the paying in book.

Petty cash

The other cash transactions will mainly be small items such as the purchase of nails or screws, fuel, travel or subsistence charges. It is best to write up each item on a petty cash slip, as illustrated below, which should be supported wherever possible by a receipt from the supplier.

Petty cash book

The transactions can then be written up from the petty cash slips into a petty cash book week by week. The total weekly expenditure will be funded by a cheque from the current bank account either to reimburse out of pocket payments or to maintain the petty cash allowance or 'float' at a constant level.

Petty Cash Voucher

Folio_____

Date_____ 19

For what required	AMOUNT	
	£	P

Signature_____

Passed by_____

Chapter Three
Money as a Measuring Rod

Money as a measuring rod. What a balance sheet cannot show. Accounts as an analytical tool. Starting capital. Fixed and current assets. Fixed and current liabilities. Ratio of current assets to current liabilities.

THE UNIVERSAL RAW MATERIAL

Own money at risk

The difference between working for yourself and working for someone else is that it is your own money which is at risk. A site foreman or even a contracts manager does not need to know much about the basic principles of accounting. He knows that there are certain forms which have to be filled in, that certain procedures have to be carried out and that his costs have to be kept within certain limits.

Initial worth

When someone decides to start up a building business, he will probably start by working out what cash he has at home and in the bank, the value of his house and whether he will be able to borrow money against it and any other valuable assets he may own, such as a motor car. In short, he will want to know what he is worth.

Universal raw material

It should be quite easy to work out what he is worth before
he goes into business, and it is sensible to do this to find out
how much he can afford to invest in the business. For money
is the first resource that will be needed in order to establish
his business. Money will be needed for an office, for office
furniture and equipment, for books of account, stationery
and files. Later money will be needed for tools, for materials
and components and for wages for skilled and unskilled
workers. In fact money can be viewed as a raw material of
business itself, and in a sense money is the universal raw
material.

Starting off in business

So to start off in business a person must either have money,
borrow money or be in a position to negotiate credit arrangements with suppliers or an overdraft arrangement with the
local bank. He will have to calculate how much ready cash
he has available to commit to his business, to which he can
add any useful assets, such as a van or a pick-up truck, which
could be used directly in the business.

Don't underestimate needs

The great mistake made by many small businessmen is to
underestimate their need for capital, hoping that they will
make big profits quickly and keep their creditors happy for a
few weeks until the money comes in. This is a bad way to
start, and such a person would be better advised to delay his
start in business for a year or two until he has some hope of
going about it in a businesslike way with adequate finance.
He should also remember that, unless he operates through a
limited company, all his assets are at risk and the failure of
his business could lead to the loss of his home, his money and
all his other assets.

Cash transformed

The money with which the business starts will be trans-
formed into other resources as trading commences. Money
will be turned into tools and account books, concrete blocks
and cement, time and labour of employees and sub-contractors. Then as work progresses, interim payments will be
received from clients and at last the first job will be finished,
so that the results of all this work will be shown in cash units.

Will it increase?

If the business has been efficient and successful, the total assets of the business will have increased and the business will be shown to be profitable. Hopefully more cash will be available so that the next project can be a little more ambitious. But whether the business is successful or not, eventually there has to be a reckoning and the 'balance sheet' will show the contractor's financial health in the same way that a thermometer records his temperature and gives an indication of his physical health.

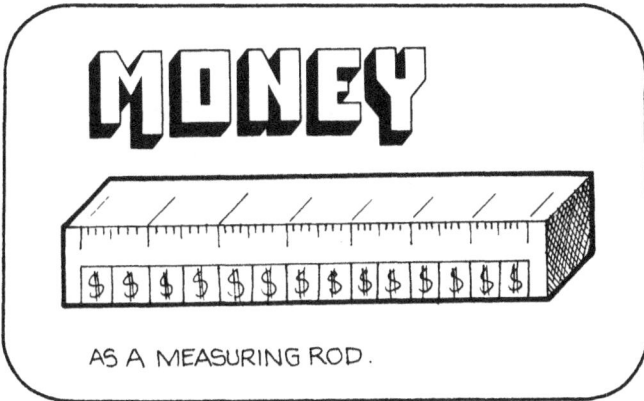

AS A MEASURING ROD.

Thus money is in a sense a measuring rod against which the success of failure of a business can be judged. For the activities of a business are mostly directed to the aim, however long term, of increasing the capital of the proprietor. Thus their effect on the prosperity of the business must be measurable, possibly indirectly, in currency units.

Accountancy: measuring effects of activities

It is necessary for the contractor to grasp some of the fundamental ideas of accounting in order to understand the way in which money is used in his business. He should see accounting as the language of business, he must be able to 'speak' this language if he is to make himself understood in the business world. If he understands it well, he should be able to forecast and measure the effects of his various business activities, and take better decisions as a result.

A simple example

Suppose a would-be contractor owns a second-hand pick-up truck worth $1000 and has cash available to start his business of $500. This means his starting capital is $1500. He tenders for a small job a sum of $300 and is awarded the contract. He spends $200 on materials and $40 on fuel and casual labour to help with the work. This means he has $60 left to cover overheads, depreciation and profit.

This example is very simple and the figures are easy to remember. But most building businesses involve dozens of transactions, large and small, each day and no-one could be expected to remember them all and work them out in his head. If anyone was foolish enough to try to get by without proper accounting, it is easy to see the muddle that his finances would get into. The trouble is that many builders do try to get by without proper accounting, with the result that in most countries more building businesses go bankrupt than any other category.

Money measurement

We must remember that if we are to accept that money is to be our measuring rod, we will get a factual valuation of the business. But some facts cannot be accurately measured in money terms and there is no way of guessing them from printed balance sheet. This is a particularly important thing to remember if you are thinking about buying someone else's business.

Method of valuation

If it has been prepared properly, a balance sheet will show the value of property and assets owned by the business, such as buildings, land, materials, equipment and work in progress, although the method of valuation needs to be examined. For example the value of work in progress will assume that the business will continue and the contracts will all be completed. But if the business was to cease immediately due to liquidation or bankruptcy, these assets would be swallowed up by the liquidated damages claimed by clients. On the other hand, property may be shown quite properly at cost price, whereas its current value may be much higher due to general inflation.

SOME THINGS A **BALANCE SHEET** CANNOT SHOW

A NEW COMPETITOR

OWNER HAS FALLEN ILL

GOOD REPUTATION

Non-monetary factors

Some of the things that a balance sheet cannot possibly show can only be judged by personal knowledge. For example a firm may have been very profitable because it has had no competition in its locality for years, but a competitor may start up next week and force it to cut its profit margins to stay in business. Or it may be that the man who ran the business has fallen ill and will no longer be able to run it so well. On the other hand the business may have gradually built up a good reputation for competence and good value, with the result that it will shortly be asked to tender for a large and potentially lucrative contract.

Practical experience

None of the above possibilities mean that it is not worth bothering to produce accounts. It just means that, as in building itself, practical experience is needed in addition to theoretical knowledge, so that the weakness of theory can be allowed for.

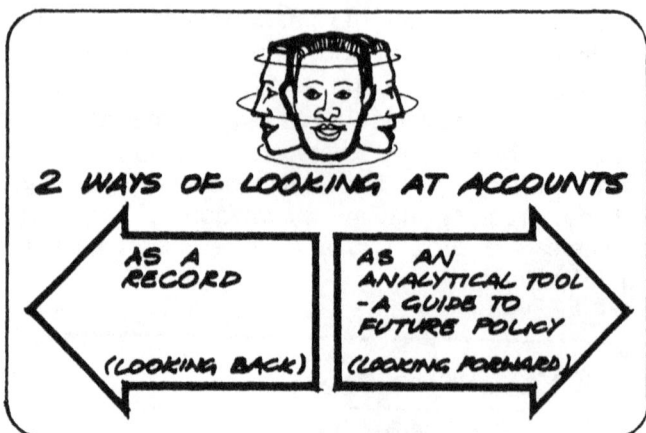

2 WAYS OF LOOKING AT ACCOUNTS

AS A RECORD (LOOKING BACK)

AS AN ANALYTICAL TOOL - A GUIDE TO FUTURE POLICY (LOOKING FORWARD)

Keeping records

There are two ways of looking at accountancy, and two ways in which accounts can help the businessman. Firstly it is a way of keeping records of monetary transactions in a systematic way. It means that you can look back into the past and say to yourself: yes I did pay the blockmaker for the supplies in June and the receipt is filed as proof: oh, but I forgot to pay this dealer in the month that payment for a load of cement was due — and so on.

Analysing accounts

The second way of looking at accounting is more dynamic. It can be described as analytical. One doesn't simply look back at transactions long after they are finished, one tries to learn lessons from them and plan for the future. This way of using accounts is still fairly new. It is sometimes known as management accountancy, because it means that accountancy becomes a tool to assist in the formulation of business policy.

The accountant's job

Let us look at the job of the accountant, remembering that in a small firm it may have to be done by the proprietor himself. His first job is to ensure that proper books of account are kept by the firm, based on full documentation and showing clearly and accurately a record of the financial transactions carried out on its behalf. From these records the accountant will prepare an annual balance sheet and profit and loss account at the end of the financial year, as well as interim accounts as and when required.

'Keeping records' approach

In the 'keeping records' approach to accountancy, this is where the accountant's job stops. In many businesses this is the case. A variety of work is obtained, the jobs are carried out and at the end of twelve months the accountant prepares a balance sheet. It may even show a modest profit compared with that of the previous year and the proprietors are quite contented.

Will never grow really fast

But such a business will never grow really fast, for the simple reason that it has no way of knowing what it does well and what it does badly. Let us look at an example right outside the building industry.

Example

There was once a business which consisted of a restaurant and a shop which specialised in food sales. The accounts covered the whole business and the proprietor did not worry too much about financial matters, despite a gradually declining series of annual profits.

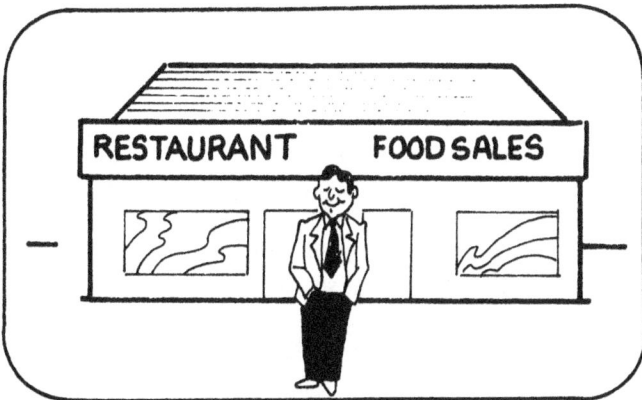

Profits vanished

Eventually the profits vanished altogether, and he began to think seriously about closing the business down completely. First he thought he would talk it over with an accountant friend to see if he could suggest anything.

Costs and overheads

His friend said he would call round and take a look at the books. He analysed the costs and overheads of the two parts of the business separately and compared them with their share of the profits.

Profits hidden

It turned out that the restaurant was doing even more badly than he thought, with payments for meals only just covering staff costs. But the shop was in fact a very profitable concern and, had he owned that alone, he would by then have received such good profits over the years that he could have opened other shops elsewhere. These profits were hidden by the losses incurred by the restaurant.

Learned his lesson

He learned his lesson quickly and closed the restaurant down straight away. A few years later he became a rich man, owning a chain of food shops.

Relevance to building

It may be said that this man was very foolish. If he had studied his business properly he would have known what was happening to it. But the point of the story is that it was only by the proper use of accounting that the lesson was learnt. Although this story was taken from a business far removed from building or civil engineering, it contains a lesson for every contractor.

Contractor's problems

Many contractors also make their own concrete blocks. Accounting can tell them whether it would be cheaper to buy. Other contractors hire concrete mixers or trucks when they are needed. Accounting could tell them whether it would be better to buy their own. Some contractors construct roads as well as building houses or roads. Accounting could tell them whether one of these activities is being heavily subsidised by the others, and guide them in realistic tendering for future projects.

You must know

It is because accounting is so important to any business-man and particularly to the building contractor that it cannot be left entirely to a professional accountant or auditor. Just as contractors have to know in principle how to construct a building, and to be aware of the difficulties and problems that can be involved, so they should, as businessmen, know how to keep accounts and construct a balance sheet and profit and loss account. What is more they should know how to interpret them to guide their business policy.

Employing capital

When a man works for an employer, his capital needs are very limited. If he is a carpenter, he may be required to supply his own tools, and the same might apply to the motor mechanic. The clerk will only have to buy himself a fountain pen!

The only money he has at risk is his weekly or monthly wages. But the man who starts his own business is faced with the need to spend money with no guarantee that it will be recovered. Thus he owes it to himself, his family, and even to his employees, to manage his capital resources effectively.

Spending money

When your savings are in a bank account, provided the bank can be relied upon, your money can come to no harm.

Vulnerable

But when your savings have been converted into a lorry, two concrete mixers, a blockmaking machine, a variety of small hand tools, four tons of cement and a pile of timber — it is much more vulnerable. The lorry may break down or be stolen, the concrete mixer may not be cleaned out by careless workers, the cement may be ruined by rain and the timber may catch fire.

Money at hazard

Of course, the contractor can obtain insurance cover against some of those possibilities. But there are less obvious dangers. Work may be taken on at the wrong price, too much money may be spent on equipment leaving too little to pay the workmen at the end of the week. If the book-keeping is left to an employee, money may be taken from the business without the owner knowing.

Understand accounting
With all these dangers, there is a clear need for the building contractor to understand basic accounting and finance. Also this knowledge will bring greater confidence if he approaches a bank manager to borrow money.

Accounts as watchdog
But more important, if his accounting is properly done, his books of accounts will become a faithful watchdog and will warn him when something is going wrong. But just as the deaf man gets no value from a watchdog — because it barks but cannot be heard, so the contractor who does not understand accounting may not understand the warning hidden in his annual accounts.

How?
Now that we have discussed why accounting is important let us begin to think about *how* it is done.

Keep business accounts separate
The first thing to remember is that the accounts for the business must be kept separate from those of the owner, even if he has no partners and has unlimited liability if things go wrong. This is, among other reasons, to allow comparison between one year's trading and the next for tax purposes, and to provide accounts for a distinct business unit in the event of the owner wishing to raise a loan or sell a part of the business.

Only report effects on business
For example, a contractor may withdraw $200 from his business and, although he will be no better or worse off personally as a result, this transaction will have to be shown in the accounts of the business. This is because, although the contractor is just as well off as before, the assets of the business have been reduced by $200. Thus a transaction can have one effect as far as the owner is concerned and a different effect on the business. The financial accounts of the business will report only the effects of transactions on the business.

Starting capital

The first decision that has to be faced by the new building contractor will be the decision as to how much starting capital he will require. He will have to work out how much money will be expended on wages and materials before payment is received from the client.

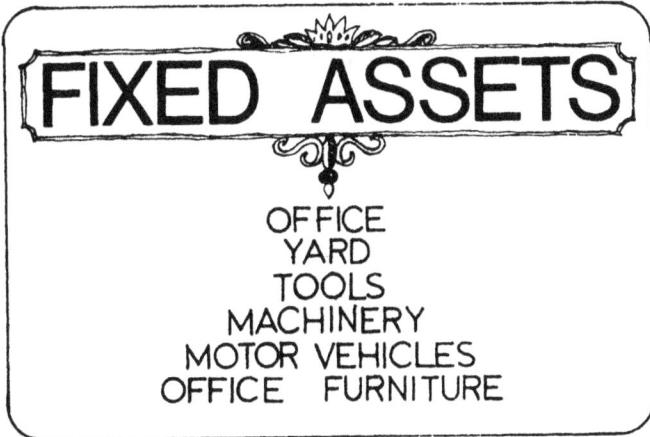

FIXED ASSETS

OFFICE
YARD
TOOLS
MACHINERY
MOTOR VEHICLES
OFFICE FURNITURE

Fixed assets

He will also have to work out his requirements for an office, a yard, tools and possibly machinery and motor vehicles. In accountant's language, these are known as fixed assets whether or not they are in fact fixed to the ground. Fixed in this sense means that money employed in this way will not usually be released unless the business is closed down or reduced in size.

CURRENT ASSETS

WORK IN PROGRESS
MATERIALS ON SITE
DEBTORS

Current assets

The rest of the money in the business which goes to pay wages and materials to finance jobs until payment is received is known as "current assets" because it is circulating in the business. It is like the money which finances stock on the grocer's shelves — one day it may be turned into tinned food — and then be sold later in the week and turned back into money — then it may be used to buy vegetables which will hopefully be sold quickly to produce money again.

Thus the money tied up on current assets for the builder — *work in progress, materials* for future jobs, money owed by *debtors* for past work — can be expected to turn up as cash in the reasonably near future.

Fixed assets or working capital?

Not many contractors start off in the happy position of simply deciding how much money is needed to start off their business. In most cases they start off with a very limited sum of money knowing that, if things go wrong, no more will be available to cope with the emergency. This means that there has to be a direct choice between money for fixed assets and money for current assets or working capital.

Caution

Working capital can easily be converted into fixed assets. But selling property etc. to turn fixed assets back into cash is much more difficult at short notice. Thus it is best to be cautious at first and limit investment in property and plant, making quite sure that enough money is available to cope with the day-to-day financing of the business.

Liabilities

Just as there are current assets and fixed assets, so most established businesses have current liabilities and fixed liabilities. As with assets, the liabilities represent debts owed by the *business,* which may not be the same thing as the debts owed by the owner of the business.

Fixed liabilities

Fixed liabilities are debts which are owed by the business but which will not have to be paid in the immediate future. For example, a relative may offer a loan to get the business started on the understanding that it will not have to be repaid for at least five years or the bank may agree to a fixed term loan. In addition the owner's initial capital comes under the heading of fixed liabilities, because it is owed by the business *to the owner* of the business.

Assets equal liabilities

It is a basic principle of accounting that every asset has an equivalent liability. Since the business and its owner are separate legal entities, the owner's capital which is an *asset* as far as he is concerned is a *liability from the standpoint of the business.*

Current liabilities

Current liabilities are the most common form of liabilities in a new business. They represent debts which will (or may) have to be repaid in the immediate future. Examples are creditors, since most suppliers of such things as building materials, even if they give credit, expect to be paid at the end of the month in which a statement is sent. Employees naturally expect to be paid at the end of the week. The tax authorities will not wait when payments fall due. Even a bank overdraft represents a *current* liability although it may continue to operate up to an agreed limit for quite a long period. This is because the bank has the right to demand repayment at any time, so it comes under the headings of debts that *may* have to be paid at short notice.

Current Liabilities
(Owed by company)

e.g.
CREDITORS :- Materials Merchants
                 Plant Hire Firms
TAX PAYMENTS
BANK OVERDRAFTS

Keep current liabilities under control

Since the contractor knows that current liabilities will have to be repaid in quite a short time, it is important to keep them under quite strict control.

Ratio of current assets to liabilities

Thus one of the key measures of the health of a company is the ratio of current assets to current liabilities. For if a company will shortly have to make heavy payments, but has no reasonable prospects of obtaining money from others to cover them — serious problems lie ahead!

Minimum ratio

In general the higher the ratio, the safer will the company be in the event of difficulty. Of course there is no point in having cash in the business for no purpose, but it is wise to aim at a certain minimum ratio so that there will always be cash available in an emergency.

The best ratio for any particular firm must be decided in accordance with its own trading pattern. However as a general rule, current assets should be at least twice current liabilities.

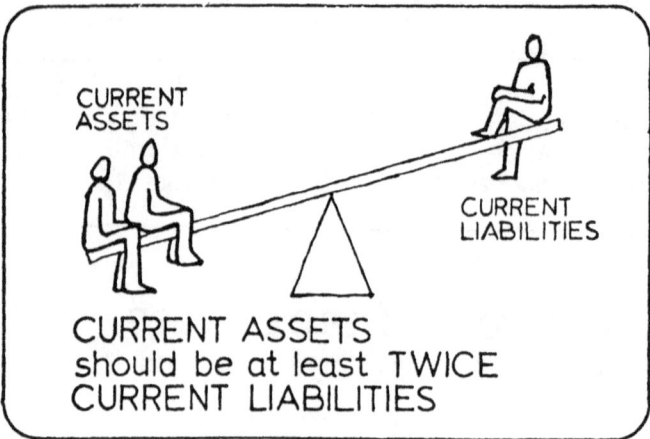

CURRENT ASSETS

CURRENT LIABILITIES

CURRENT ASSETS
should be at least TWICE
CURRENT LIABILITIES

Chapter Four
Basic Book-keeping

Organising information. Reasons for book-keeping. Principle of double-entry. Account entries. Debit and credit. Personal and impersonal accounts. Real and nominal accounts. The journal. Typical transactions. The cash book. Treatment of discounts. Monthly balances. Control of petty cash. Purchases book. Sales book. Wages calculations.

Organising information
Documentation is the first stage in finding out how much profit (or loss) the business is making. But documentation alone is not enough. The information contained in all the individual documents, forms and receipts has to be organised into a system so that it can be understood.

Book-keeping
The first stage in organising this information is known as book-keeping. Book-keeping for most ordinary day-to-day transactions is basically the same for most types of businesses, although there are some variations according to the size and type of the business and the form of ownership. Book-keeping for partnerships and limited companies is slightly more complicated than for a firm owned by one person alone, since a transaction involving one partner (such as drawing or providing capital) will affect the other partners.

Reasons for book-keeping
The job of the book-keeping system is to provide answers to questions that might be asked by the owners of the business or others, such as people who trade with it, the bank manager or the tax inspector, who have a right to know what is going on.

Six questions
There are six main questions to which one is likely to need answers:

1. How much money has been spent on the business by the owner(s)?

2. What has it been spent on?
3. How much money has been received from customers and clients?
4. What has this been spent on?
5. How much money is owed to other people or firms?
6. How much is owed by others to the business?

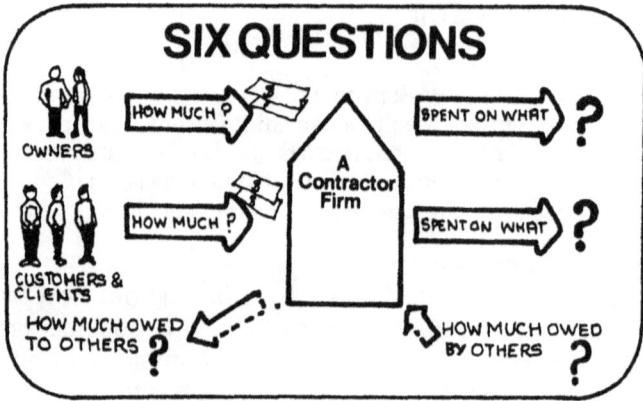

SIX QUESTIONS

OWNERS — HOW MUCH ? — A Contractor Firm — SPENT ON WHAT ?

CUSTOMERS & CLIENTS — HOW MUCH ? — SPENT ON WHAT ?

HOW MUCH OWED TO OTHERS ? — HOW MUCH OWED BY OTHERS ?

The accountant

In order to be able to answer these questions promptly and accurately whenever they are asked, it is necessary to set up a series of accounts to keep track of various aspects of the business. In its simplest form, each account consists of a large T. The title of the account is written above the T. Increases in the account are written in on the left-hand side of the vertical line. Decreases in the account are written in on the right-hand side of the vertical line.

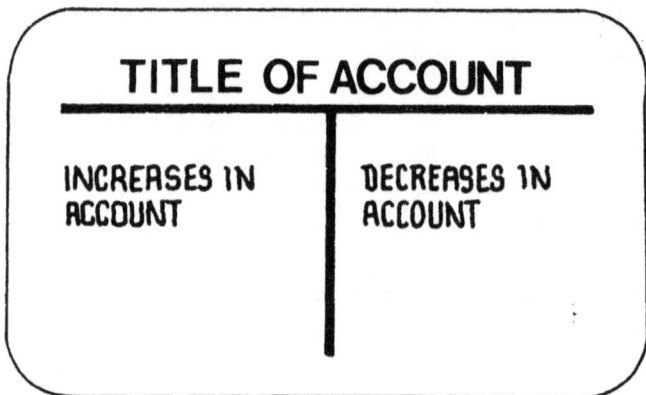

TITLE OF ACCOUNT

INCREASES IN ACCOUNT | DECREASES IN ACCOUNT

Principle of double entry

In a sense every account represents a little mini-business, with which the overall firm has some form of trading or commercial relationship. It is a general rule that whenever an entry is made in one account, an equal and opposite entry must be made in one of the other accounts. Thus if a business buys $50 worth of timber from a supplier, the materials account must show that the business has $50 worth more of assets and the supplier's account must show that the business owes him $50 on account of materials supplied. It is because of this principle of making two entries for each transaction that conventional book-keeping is sometimes described as double-entry book-keeping.

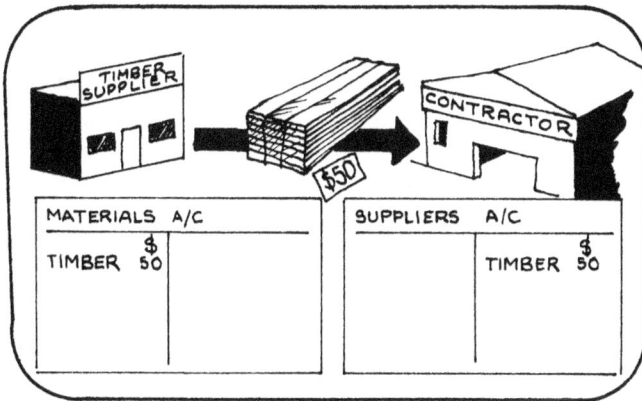

Kaburu builders

This principle applies right from the start. Let us suppose a man called John Kaburu decides to set up a contracting business called Kaburu Builders. We are of course interested not in the personal accounts of Mr Kaburu, but on the way in which his business develops and its financial results. He may decide to start his business with savings of $1,000 and a pick-up truck which has been valued at $1,200.

Which accounts?

The first thing is to decide which accounts need to be opened in order to be able to describe this action in correct book-keeping terms. Since the accounts cover Kaburu Builders, the books must show the assets now owned by the firm and the fact that it is indebted to Mr Kaburu for providing them.

Three accounts

To deal with this initial transaction we will have to open three separate accounts:

1. Cash Account
2. Plant and Vehicles Purchase Account
3. Capital Account — John Kaburu.

Capital Account

The Capital Account is an important one, since it represents the business dealings with its owner — from the point of view of the business. Newcomers to accounting sometimes find this point hard to grasp, since the owner by definition owns the business anyway. But the principle of double entry must apply even here and, since the business is about to benefit from cash and goods to the value of $2,200, there must be an equal and opposite series of entries in another account to show that $2,200 has been received by the business and is owing to the owner.

Cash transaction

The $1,000 cash transaction will affect the Cash Account and the Capital Account. As far as the Cash Account is concerned the $1,000 represents an *increase.* Thus it must appear on the left-hand side of the account. But the J. Kaburu Capital Account must see this transaction in a different light, since it has resulted in a sum of $1,000 being owed to J. Kaburu. Thus it must appear on the right-hand side of the account.

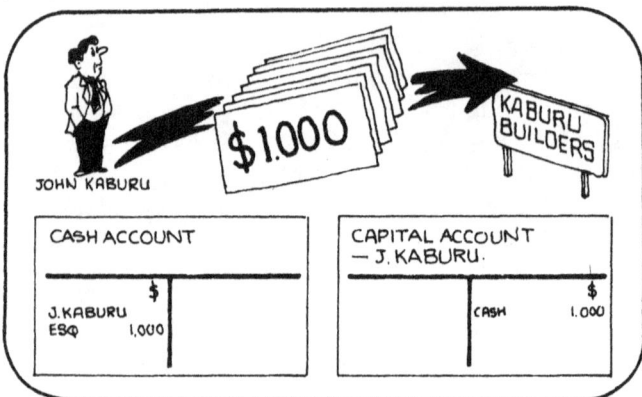

Pick-up truck

The transfer of the pick-up truck will not affect the Cash Account at all, but it will affect the Plant and Vehicles Purchase Account. From the point of view of that account, things will be better since there is an increase in the type of assets in which it is interested. This increase means that the sum of $1,200 representing the value of the pick-up truck should be entered on the left-hand side of the account. But once again the J. Kaburu Capital Account sees things in a different way. A further sum of $1,200 is now owed by the business to J. Kaburu, and so this sum of $1,200 must be shown on the right-hand side of the account.

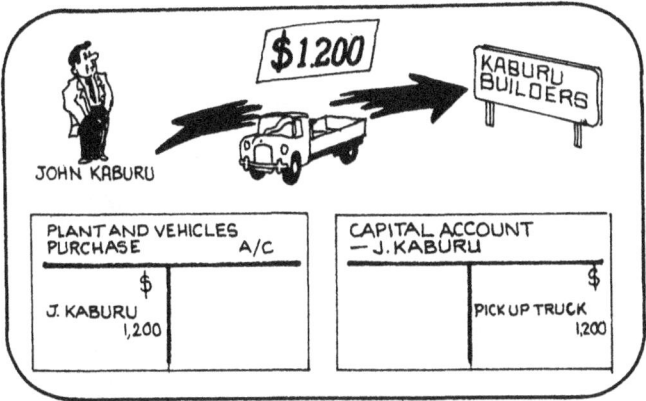

Bank account

Let us now suppose that Kaburu Builders negotiates a bank account with the local branch of the National Bank. The proprietor wisely decides to place $950 in the current account at the bank for safe keeping, leaving $50 for cash purchases. This means that we must open yet another account, called National Bank.

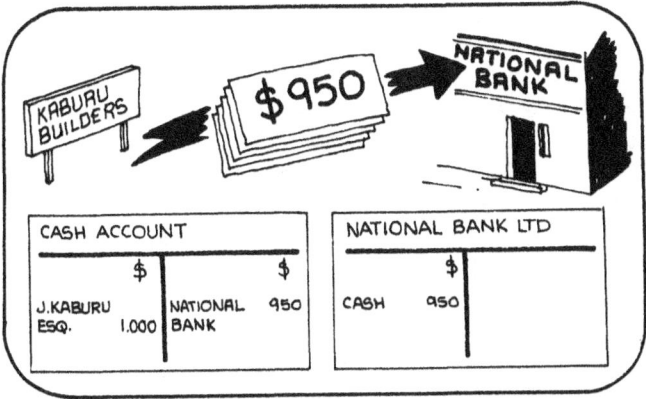

Account entries

Although the business as a whole will be neither better nor worse off financially now, the two relevant accounts see things differently. The Cash Account has been decreased, so an entry of $950 must appear on the right-hand side. The new National Bank Account however is now better off to the tune of $950, so an entry of $950 must appear on the left-hand side of that account.

Debit and credit

As a reminder of the meaning of entries on either side of the vertical line of the 'T', a 'Dr' is sometimes shown on the left of the T and a 'Cr' is shown on the right. These stand for debit and credit. In the special language of accounting, the left-hand side of an account is known as the debit side. The right-hand side is known as the credit side.

Debit and credit entries

Value received, belonging to or owing to the business must always appear on the debit side, and each entry on that side is known as a debit entry. Value given out or owing to other persons or firms is entered on the credit side, and each entry on that side is known as a credit entry.

Checking up

Whenever one needs to check up on the state of any particular account, it is simply a matter of adding up the debit entries and the credit entries and subtracting the smaller total from the larger total. If the total of the entries on the debit side is the greater, the account is said to have a debit balance. If the total of the entries on the credit side is the greater, the account is said to have a credit balance.

Ledger

The collection of individual accounts relating to a business is known as a ledger. A small firm might keep all its separate accounts in a single general ledger. A larger firm would have a whole series of ledgers, with each one covering a group of accounts. A ledger need not be a thick, heavily bound book. For many purposes, a set of loose leaf pages is more convenient so that additional accounts can be introduced as trading develops.

Classification

It is convenient to attempt some form of classification of

accounts within the overall ledger system. The first division can be made between personal accounts and impersonal accounts.

Personal accounts

Personal accounts cover not only transactions with individuals, but also transactions with business or other entities, such as firms, companies, local authorities or government ministries. In general a letter written by any person or organisation to the business would give rise to a personal account if it entered into a financial transaction with the business concerned.

Impersonal accounts

Impersonal accounts cover other aspects of the business, and in turn can be subdivided into *real* accounts and *nominal* accounts.

Real accounts

Real accounts cover dealings in or ownership of property or other assets which may be needed in order to conduct the business. Some examples are:

Land
Buildings
Cash
Materials
Plant and machinery
Tools
Furniture and office equipment
Motor vehicles

Nominal accounts

Nominal accounts cover expenses, income, losses and gains. They generally cover those expenses which do not result in the purchase of tangible assets, but do cover services and general business expenses. Examples are:

Wages and salaries
Rents
Insurance
Telephone
Interest on loans
Repairs
Depreciation
Bad debts
Discounts.

IMPERSONAL ACCOUNTS

REAL ACCOUNTS   NOMINAL ACCOUNTS

Contracts ledger

In a building business, it may be helpful to have a separate set of cost accounts relating to individual jobs or contracts. If this system is adopted, a separate account can be set up for each contract showing costs on the debit side and income on the credit side. This system has the great advantage that the contractor can tell which jobs are profitable and which give rise to losses, and adjust his tendering policy accordingly.

Subsidiary books

There is a preliminary stage in book-keeping before the ledger accounts are written up. The account books which enable this to be done are sometimes called subsidiary books or books of original entry. These subsidiary books include the journal, cash book, sales book and purchases book.

Subsidiary first

It is a general rule that no entry should appear in any ledger unless it has first been recorded in a subsidiary book of some kind.

The journal

The journal is something like a diary of financial transactions of a business. All transactions, including both payments and receipts, should be entered in the journal on the day that they take place, so that there is no danger of them being forgotten.

A complete story

Each journal entry tells a complete story of one financial transaction, including instructions as to how it should be entered in the ledger accounts. Thus for each transaction the journal has to show:

1. The date
2. Particulars of the transaction
3. The effects of the transaction on the ledger accounts.

Kaburu builders

Returning to John Kaburu and his new firm Kaburu Builders, we remember he started by transferring $1,000 in cash and a pick-up truck worth $1,200 to the business. The journal must show the effect of this on the various ledger accounts, remembering that there will be both debit and credit entries, and that these must add up to the same total on both sides.

These entries are shown below as entered in a typical journal. On the left-hand side the date is entered, together with particulars of the transaction. On the right-hand side there is the typical 'T' of an account with debit entries on the left and credit entries on the right of the vertical line. The remaining column, labelled 'folio', shows which ledger account each item is to be entered in. The codes can be chosen to suit the individual business, but these are as follows:

R1 — Real Account No.1 (Cash)
R2 — Real Account No.2 (Motor Vehicles)
PL — Private Ledger (Capital Account — J. Kaburu)

JOURNAL

1978	OPENING ENTRIES		Folio	Dr. (Assets)	Cr (Liabilities)
1st March.	CASH IN HAND	Dr	R1	1,000	
	MOTOR VEHICLES	Dr	R2	1,200	
	TO CAPITAL		PL		2,200
				2,200	2,200.
	BEING THE ASSETS AND LIABILITIES OF KABURU BUILDERS ON 1st MARCH 1978.				

Balance

It will be seen that the total of debit and credit entries is the same, thus maintaining the principle of a balance between the two columns, which leads eventually to that basic business statement — the balance sheet.

Practice

Although the entries may seem a little complicated, after a certain amount of practice it should become routine to decide which ledger accounts will be affected by individual transactions.

Writing a cheque

Thus if Mr Kaburu writes a cheque (from the Kaburu Builders account) to a supplier of building materials who has supplied timber on credit, the account with the bank must be

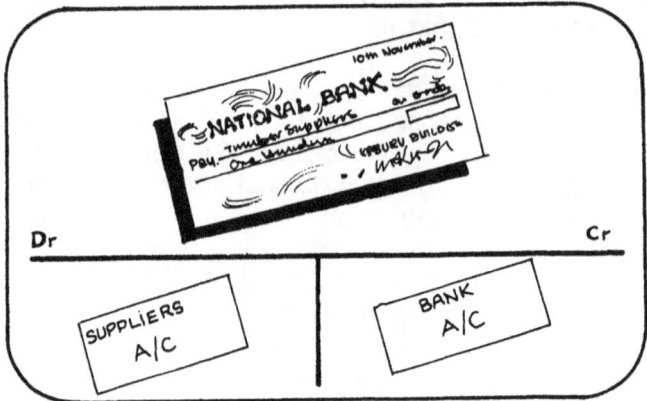

credited with that sum. This is because the bank will now have less of Kaburu Builders' money and so owes less on its account. The supplier's account will be debited with an equal sum to show that the debt has been discharged.

Purchase for cash

If Mr Kaburu buys some tools or materials for cash (other

than small purchases for petty cash), the purchasers account must be debited to show that the firm now possesses these goods. Equally the cash account (or cash book) must be credited to show that there is now less money available in the business.

Accounts to clients

Most building contracts involve the contractor in offering credit to the client, although there may be arrangements for monthly interim payments during the course of the contract. Whenever an interim or final account is issued to the client or his representative, it is necessary to credit the sales account to show that a sale has been made. Equally the client's account must be debited to show that he owes the appropriate sum; this is now an additional asset to the firm in the form of a debt due.

Credit control

The client's accounts can be helpful to the contractor in credit control, since they will show how long the client takes to pay his debts after he receives and checks interim or final accounts.

Purchase on credit

Once Kaburu Builders has been recognized as a trading concern, it should be possible to get suppliers to agree to provide credit on purchases of building materials up to an agreed limit. This will mean that a whole series of credit purchases will need to be entered up in the journal. In each case it will be necessary to debit the purchaser's account that the goods are now in the hands of the business. The account of the supplier must be credited to show that he has a valid debt due which will have to be paid over to him in due course.

PURCHASE OF GOODS ON CREDIT

Dr

PURCHASES ACCOUNT

Cr

SUPPLIERS A/C

Other transactions

There are of course many other types of transaction, but further practice and thought should allow the correct entries in the ledger accounts to be indicated.

Journal example

Let us suppose that Kaburu Builders gets its first job, the painting and renovation of a market stall and that he has been able to obtain credit from Manake Building Supplies Ltd. for his purchases of materials. His ledger at the end of the contract may be as illustrated below:

CASH ACCOUNT	
£	£
J. Kaburu Esq. 1000	National Bank 950

CAPITAL A/c J.KABURU	
	£
	Cash 1000
	Pick up truck 1200

PLANT AND VEHICLES PURCHASE ACCOUNT	
£	
J.Kaburu Esq. 1200	

NATIONAL BANK LTD.	
£	£
Cash 950	Petty Cash 100

PURCHASES ACCOUNT	
£	
Manake B.S. 280	
Manake B.S. 60	

MANAKE BUILDING SUPPLIES LTD.			
	£		£
Cheque	340	Timber, etc.	280
		Paint	60

Cash book

The cash book comes under the heading of subsidiary books, although it also contains some of the information to be found in the ledger and is in fact the cash account of the business.

Cash and cheques

Although the description 'cash book' is in common use, it is rather misleading because it is used to record transactions with the bank using the cheque book and paying in book as well as cash transactions. An example is shown below:

Dr.   **Typical Cash Book Page**   Cr.

DATE	PARTICULARS	FOLIO	DISCOUNT	CASH	BANK	DATE	PARTICULARS	FOLIO	DISCOUNT	CASH	BANK

Two parts

Since payments are both made and received in a business, the cash book is divided into two parts with a double vertical line to separate them. On the left-hand side all receipts of cash into the business are shown, including the owner's capital and loans as well as payments from clients for work done. On the right-hand side expenses and payments from the business are shown.

Discounts

There are separate columns for discounts, since it is a common trading practice to allow a discount of 2½% or 5% for promptly paid accounts. It is important that these columns should be filled in correctly as, when discounts are allowed, settlements will be different from the figures for credit transactions already written into the books.

Client's payments

If a client or customer pays for a job by cheque, the value of the cheque should be entered in the 'Bank' column on the left-hand side. If the payment is made in cash and kept in the office cash box, it should be entered in the 'Cash' column. If, however, a client's cash payment is paid into the firm's bank account, it should be entered in the 'Bank' column.

Monthly balances

It is common practice to balance account books on a monthly basis. Thus the cash book illustrated above starts with an entry showing the balances of cash in hand and at the bank on the left-hand side. The balances carried forward to the following month are shown at the foot of the columns on the right-hand side.

Petty cash book

In order to keep small transactions, such as the purchase of postage stamps, from cluttering up the main cash book, most businesses also have a petty cash book. Most building jobs re-require occasional small purchases and payments for casual labour, etc. Thus it may be necessary to have a separate petty cash book on each site under the control of the foreman.

Balance or float

It would be unreasonable to expect an employee to finance site expenses out of his own pocket, so it is normal to allow him a certain cash balance or 'float' from which to make payments. This float is brought up to its original level regularly (normally every week or every month), when the holder of the float is required to account for the payments he has made.

Control of petty cash

In many small businesses most of the financial records are kept by the owner. The petty cash book (or books) is the exception. If every site foreman had to wait until the owner turned up to buy a bag of nails the work would fall behind. In addition the keeping of petty cash records is time-consuming, and it is natural to want to leave it to an employee. However the owner must remember that employees are human and some (certainly not all) may be tempted to augment their wages by falsifying their petty cash returns.

Two forms of cheating

An employee can cheat his employer on petty cash in two main ways. First he could pretend that he made payments on behalf of the firm which he did not in fact make. Secondly he could falsify the information in the petty cash book and borrow from his 'float'.

Checking

Thus the owner should regularly check the petty cash books of his employees. He needs to check that the petty cash slips are accompanied by receipts or at least that the purchases seem reasonable. He should check that the records are written up properly and that additions have been carried out correctly. To discourage borrowing from the float he should ask to see the cash in hand occasionally, and not always at regular intervals. Finally he should see that the float is not larger than necessary.

Typical entries

A common type of petty cash book with typical entries is shown below:

Petty Cash Book

DATE	REC'D	DATE	PARTICULARS	Vr. No.	TOTAL EXPENDED	POSTAGE	STAT-IONERY	CASUAL LABOUR	FUEL	MATERIALS	SUNDRY
b/fd	5.00	3.3	Stamps	3/1	0.55	0.55					
1.3	15.00	8.3	Stationery	3/2	1.10		1.10				
		15.3	Casual labour	3/3	5—			5—			
		21.3	Petrol for mixer	3/4	4—				4—		
		22.3	Nails and screws	3/5	1.28					1.28	
		23.3	Note book	3/6	1.25		1.25				
		25.3	Timber	3/7	2—					2—	
		30.3	Stamps	3/8	0.50	0.50					
					15.68						
			Balance c/d		4.32						
	20—				20.00	1.05	2.35	5—	4—	3.28	—

Like a cash book

It will be seen that the petty cash book is, as might be expected, rather like a miniature cash book. Income is shown on the left-hand side, starting with the balance in hand or brought forward (b/fd) from the previous month. The entry below that shows the cash drawn to bring the float up to the agreed level of, in this case, $20. On the right-hand side the month's expenses are listed, with each voucher (petty cash slip) numbered for easy reference. At the foot of the right-hand column, the balance of cash in hand at the end of the month is shown. This has to be brought up to the agreed float level, so that the holder of the petty cash has funds for the next monthly period.

Purchases and sales

The other two main subsidiary books which are used for original entries from basic forms, documents and vouchers are the *purchases book* and the *sales book.*

Credit only

These two books are used to record credit transactions only. Cash transactions, both purchases and sales, are recorded in the cash book.

Purchases book

The purchases book, as its name implies, is used to record all purchases of materials, tools, plant and equipment on credit.

Permanent record

Transactions should be entered up in the book regularly and, since it is needed as a permanent record, it is wise to choose a substantial hard-covered book. A typical sheet from the book is shown below.

Purchases book

DATE	NAME	DETAILS	FOLIO	COST

Invoice numbers

A column is provided for invoice numbers, so that these can easily be traced back if there is any query when the supplier's statement comes to be checked as well as for auditing purposes. A further column shows the ledger account folio number for easy reference.

Sales book

The sales book records the value of work carried out for clients and customers. The same principle applies and the name of the person or organisation concerned and the amount involved should be shown.

Permanent record

Once again it is worthwhile to buy a substantial hard-covered book, so that a permanent record will be available. A typical sheet is shown below.

Sales book

DATE	NAME	DETAILS	FOLIO	COST

Wages calculations

Wages calculations vary from one country to another according to the particular statutory deductions for tax or insurance that may be in force. The calculations will normally be based on the time sheet or daily allocation sheets submitted for the previous week, with the number of hours worked multiplied by the agreed hourly rate together with an addition for overtime. It is best to carry out these calculations in a bound wages book, and often preferable to use carbon paper to produce a duplicate copy.

Making up wage packets

Confusion is avoided by drawing the exact sum required to pay net wages from the bank in cash using an 'uncrossed' cheque. In a small firm, the contractor will himself make up the wages book, draw the cash for the wages, make up the individual wage packets and hand them over personally. Where this is not possible, it is a wise precaution to separate the duties among various members of staff, ensuring that those who enter the figures in the books do not handle the money.

Enter in cash book

The total amount of money required each week to pay wages is entered up in the cash book in the usual way.

'Posting' to ledger

All of the transactions represented as entries in the subsidiary books must be regularly written up into the appropriate ledger accounts. The technical accounting term for this is 'posting' the entries to the ledger.

Chapter Five
Analysis Sheets

Simplifying book-keeping. Using bank information. The risk of simplification. Keeping cash book for bank transactions. Difficulties with credit transactions. Payment procedures. Buying and using an analysis book. Bank statements. Checking the bank balance.

Simplifying book-keeping

In a small business, where almost all the office work has to be done by the contractor if it is done at all, it is difficult to find the time to run a complete double entry book-keeping system. Although there are always risks in simplifying book-keeping by reducing the number of books and separate accounts, it is better to do this than have a complete system not properly carried out because of shortage of time.

The absolute minimum

One way of simplifying book-keeping is to ask what is the absolute minimum number of books that need to be kept if the records are to be sufficient to produce a balance sheet and profit and loss account and to enable the contractor to trace back and explain individual transactions.

Bank information

If a bank account is operated, the staff at the bank will do some of the work for the contractor. Operating a bank account correctly provides three basic sources of information.

1. The paying-in book
2. The cheque book
3. The statement of transaction

Maximising bank transactions

Since we are looking for ways to simplify the recording of financial transactions, it is wise to maximise the number of transactions that will automatically be recorded by the bank on the contractor's behalf.

All receipts paid into bank

There is no reason why all receipts into the business should not be paid into the bank account. This means that it is possible to do without one 'cash' column in the cash book, and the receipts side of the cash book can be written up directly from the copy of the paying-in book form retained by the contractor.

Using paying-in book

In the building business most payments from customers and clients come in fairly large individual sums, which are worth banking separately as soon as they are received. They will usually be accompanied by a payment advice note, and the client's name and the reason for the payment (job number and certificate, etc.) should be noted on the contractor's copy of the paying-in book form. Any small payments for minor repairs, etc., even if they have been made in cash, can be paid in to the bank with one paying-in slip but with a note of the individual amounts on the contractor's copy.

Transfer to cash book

Thus the paying-in book becomes an important record book for the contractor, showing all payments into the business. These written notes will then be used to transfer the information to the cash book and to check the entries on the bank statement when it is sent.

The risk

The main risk in dispensing with full ledger accounts for transactions with clients is that the contractor will not have a complete and readily accessible record of amounts billed to customers but not yet paid. In a large business this would be a serious fault. But in a small business with only a few contracts running at any one time, the contractor will probably be able to remember which clients have not yet paid for work which has been billed to them.

A file tray

However, it might be a help to keep one special file tray for copies of certificates and bills which have been sent to clients but not yet paid. It is then possible to look through them occasionally to see if any are overdue. Once payment is received, the certificate or bill can be removed, marked as paid and placed in the file for that particular job.

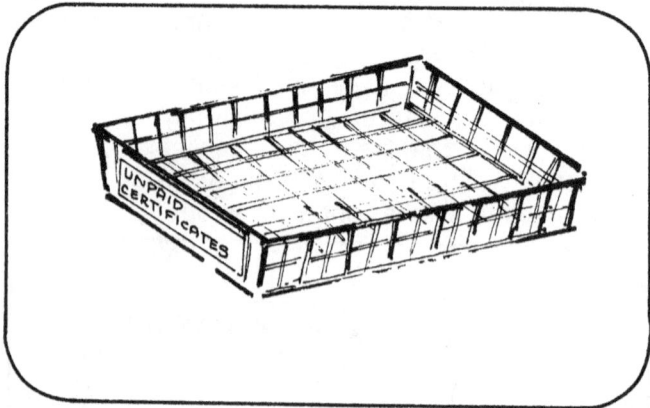

Payments

Payments from the business usually give rise to more problems for the contractor than receipts, quite apart from the problem of finding the money to make the payments! To start with it is a characteristic of the building business that the actual number of payments is usually very much greater than the number of receipts, so there is more room for error and confusion in seeing that they are all correctly recorded.

Bank account helps

Once again the bank account can be a big help in getting information properly recorded and, providing the contractor is reputable and well-known to the supplier, it will usually be possible to issue cheques to cover the larger purchases.

Less cash carried

Apart from the convenience of paying in cash for goods purchased, there is the further great advantage that the contractor does not need to carry so much cash about with him. When cash is carried, there is always the risk of losses or theft. But, if a cheque book is lost, no financial loss should result providing the bank is notified promptly.

Cheque is a receipt

An additional advantage is that in many countries a cashed cheque is accepted as legal proof of payment. So the contractor does not have to bother to get a signed receipt from the payee for every payment he makes, as he should do as a safeguard in cash transactions.

Keeping cash book for bank transactions

Providing all major payments are made by cheque, all the purchases for cash can be left to the petty cash book. This means that the cash book can in fact be used only for trans-actions through the bank account, which makes for much easier book-keeping. Providing this is done, the cash book can be entered up directly from the cheque book and paying-in book, together with any other payments (bank charges, standing orders, etc.) notified directly by or to the bank.

The cheque book

Most banks issue cheque books to their customers con-taining a number of cheques, each of which is split into two parts by perforations. The actual cheque itself is filled in and signed before being given to the payee. The other part or cheque 'stub' remains permanently in the cheque book to enable the customer to keep a record of each cheque that he has issued.

The cheque stub

Although the cheque stub is quite small, there is plenty of room to write in the three items of information contained on the cheque:

1. The date
2. The payee
3. The amount paid.

Crossings

Most cheques will be crossed /& Co./ to show that they must be paid through a bank account. When a cheque is uncrossed or crossed in a special way such as /A/c Payee Only/, this should also be noted on the stub.

Additional information

It will be helpful if this direct note of what has been written on the cheque is supplemented by additional information on the purpose of the payment. This can consist of just a few words, such as 'wages w/e 26 July', 'timber for job 62', or 'fuel for vehicles', but it will be a very great help when the entries come to be made in the cash book. In addition, the amount of any discount deducted should be noted.

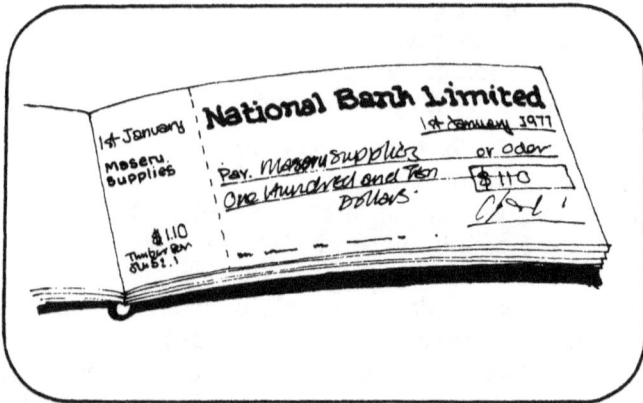

Thus the simplified pattern of book-keeping entries for a small building business would be:

Receipts — All paid into bank — In cash book

Payments — If paid by cheque — In cash book
— If paid in cash — In petty cash book.

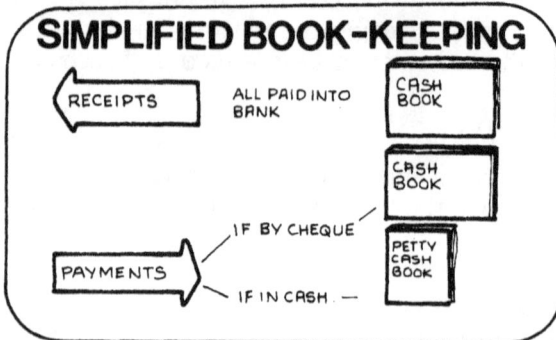

SIMPLIFIED BOOK-KEEPING

Difficulties with credit transactions

The lack of full ledger accounts will mean that it will be a little more difficult to deal with credit transactions. This is because it is necessary to check each supplier's financial statements and also extra care will have to be taken to see that settlements are made promptly when they are due. Prompt payment is important for the contractor's business reputation as well as to take advantage of trade discounts.

File trays

Once again file trays in the contractor's office can be a big help with credit transactions.

One for invoices

One file tray can take all invoices for goods supplied. In the case of direct deliveries to sites invoices should be checked against the delivery ticket sent in by the site foreman. If he has noted any shortages or breakages, the supplier should be contacted and the invoice altered accordingly.

One for unpaid statements

At the end of the month, it is the usual practice for the supplier to send a statement, showing the total of all invoices for purchases made in that month. When the statement arrives, all the invoices relating to that supplier should be checked against the statement. If any items are incorrect, the supplier should be contacted and appropriate amendments to the statement agreed. Once the statement has been agreed as correct, it can be placed in the 'unpaid statements' tray until it is due for payment. It is usually convenient to attach the relevant invoices to the statement with a pin or staple for record purposes.

After statement paid

Once the statement has been paid it can be removed from the tray. The number of the cheque and the date of payment should be noted on the statement, and it can be placed in the file relating to the appropriate supplier.

A simple system

There is now a simple system to deal with financial transactions based on information related to banking transactions together with a petty cash book. The next stage is to think about the sort of cash book that will be needed, and how it should be written up.

Buying a cash analysis book

Lined cash books are available in many shapes and sizes. Since the cash book will provide the main source of financial information for the small contractor, it is probably worthwhile to invest in a fairly heavily bound version that will stand up to reasonable wear and tear. The most suitable for the present purchase is an 'analysis' book with a number of columns as illustrated below:

Cash analysis book

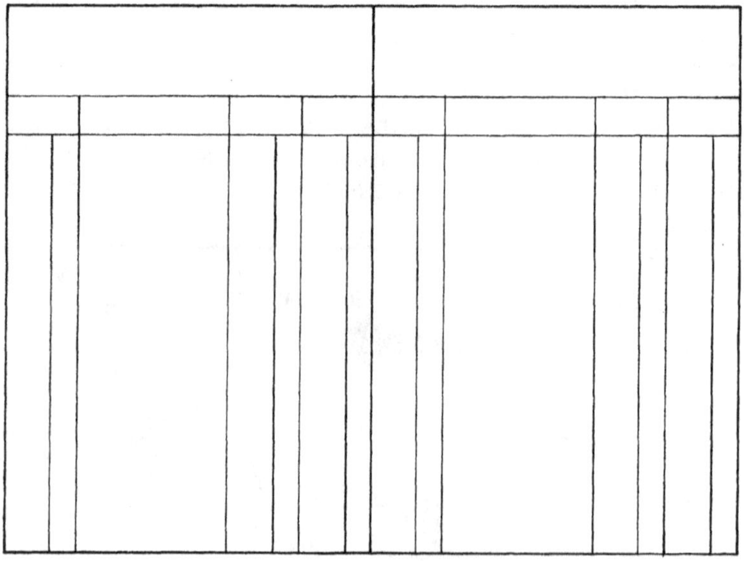

For the sake of clarity only a few of the columns are shown in the illustration.

Reason for columns

The reason for having so many columns is that it will allow the contractor to separate out expenditure under a number of headings. This will be of assistance when he comes to analyse the figures in order to produce a profit and loss account.

The receipts side

In most small building businesses the analysis on the receipts side is fairly easy. It will be necessary to separate capital brought in by the owner or his partners from 'sales and work done' which would cover all trading receipts. There may also be occasional receipts from sales of plant or equipment which would have to be separated from trading receipts. For most purposes it should be sufficient to have five columns on the receipts side.

First three columns

The first three columns would show the date, the source of the payment (the client or customer) and the amount paid into the bank. All these details should be available from the paying-in book.

Last two columns

The last two columns would be the analysis columns, labelled:

1. Sales and work done
2. Miscellaneous (Misc.)

Five columns

Thus five columns will be needed on the receipts side of the analysis book. They will be laid out as illustrated below.

ANALYSIS BOOK

RECEIPTS SIDE

1	2	3	4	5
DATE	PAYMENT FROM	TO BANK	SALES WORK DONE	MISC.

Entries in analysis columns

Every payment received by the business must be entered in one of these analysis columns. For example an interim payment on a school extension scheme would be entered under 'Sales and work done'. The funds received for the sale of a concrete mixer surplus to the firm's requirements would appear under 'Misc.'.

The Misc. column

Of course the 'Misc.' column will contain a mixture of payments which will need to be split up further when the profit and loss account is prepared. But only a small proportion of the receipts into the business will come under this 'umbrella' heading, so it should not be too difficult to sort them out when the time comes.

Splitting receipts

In most cases the complete amount received will be entered in either column 4 or column 5 and the other column will be left blank. But occasionally the sum will have to be divided between the two. One instance could be that some building work has been done for a client who happens to be a motor dealer. He has bought the contractor's second-hand pick-up truck for $250 and owes $826 for the building work. The amount shown on the cheque of $1076 will be shown in column 3. Then column 4 will show $826 and column 5 will show $250. The important rule is that the entries in columns 4 and 5 must always *total* the sum in column 3.

Example

Entries on the receipts side for a typical month might be as shown below:

1	2	3	4	5
DATE	PAYMENT FROM	TO BANK	SALES + WORK DONE	MISC.
June 4	Muringi Motors	1076	826	250
— 6	Kisumu Council	4275	4275	
— 7	H. Kirby	821	821	
— 10	Maluki Bros.	67		67
— 12	Star Hotel	428	428	
— 18	Roads Board	728	728	
— 23	Kisumu Hardware	23		23
— 27	Muringi Motors	72	72	
— 30	J. Musoke	312	312	

Numbering receipts

It may be helpful to have an additional narrow column so that all receipts can be numbered in chronological order. One quite convenient system is to have a numbering system that lasts for a full financial year. Thus receipts in 1978 would be numbered 78/1, 78/2, 78/3, etc. It is sufficient to number them 1, 2, 3, etc. in the cash analysis as this will enable them to be traced.

The payments side

Separated by a double vertical line from the receipts side of the cash analysis book is the payments side. Receipts and payments are quite independent of each other, but it is helpful to have them together on a pair of pages for each month to make analysis easier.

First three columns

The first three columns on the payments side are similar to those on the receipts side. They show the date, to whom the payment has been made (or the reason — e.g. wages) and the value of the cheque. All these details should be available from the cheque stub or, in the case of bank charges, standing orders, etc., directly from the bank.

Cheque number column

It may also be useful to have a column for the cheque number, to make it easier to refer back to the reason for the payment.

Analysis column

Since the profit and loss account will need to give a split of expenses between materials, wages, sub contractors, plant, office expenses, etc. there will need to be more analysis columns on the payments side than on the receipts side.

How many columns?

The exact number of columns required will depend on the nature of the business, since the number and type of expenses likely to be incurred depend on the variety of the work and the way in which it is to be carried out. Expenses which occur only occasionally should be entered in a Misc. column, so that the main columns can concentrate on items like wages which occur again and again.

Recurring expenses

Some of the expenses which are likely to recur and so justify separate columns are:

1. Materials
2. Wages and salaries
3. Owner's drawings (salary and fees)
4. Sub contract payments
5. Office rent and general expenses
6. Plant running expenses
7. Transport running expenses
8. Plant hire
9. Payments to petty cash account.

Separate columns

If experience shows that a number of payments is likely to be made under each of these headings during the course of most months, then it will be easier to allot separate columns to each of them. However if, for example, a contractor makes very little use of hired plant, then these occasional payments can be left to the Misc. column.

Occasional payments in Misc. column

As on the receipts side, a Misc. (miscellaneous) column can take care of occasional financial transactions as these entries can be sorted out at the stage when a profit and loss account is to be drafted. Some of these payments may be:

a. Purchase of plant and vehicles
b. Bank charges
c. Insurance
d. Printing and stationery (other than petty cash)
e. Professional fees (e.g. estimator)
f. Interest on loans
g. Advertising
h. Repayments of owner's capital.

Example

Thus a typical series of headings for the payments side of a cash analysis might be as illustrated opposite:

Most payments under one heading

Most payments will appear in only one of the analysis columns with the amount shown under the appropriate headings being the same as the value of the cheque shown in column 3. For example, a cheque to the materials supplier for $128.32 in settlement of his monthly statement would be shown in column 3 and also in column 5. A cheque to an electrical sub contractor for $150 would appear in column 3 and also in column 8.

ANALYSIS BOOK

PAYMENTS SIDE

1	2	3	4	5	6	7	8	9	10	11	12	13	14
DATE	PAID TO	CHEQUE VALUE.	№										

Splitting payments

There may be times when a payment may have to be split and entered under more than one heading. This is most likely to happen when cash is drawn from the bank for a number of purposes.

Example

For example a contractor may have the following payments to make in cash at the end of a week:

	$
Wages	212.80
Office rent	25.50
Petty cash	18.26
	256.56

This means that there will have to be four cash entries, one in the bank column (column 3) and the remainder in the analysis columns.

1	2	3	4	6	9	13	14
DATE	PAID TO	CHEQUE VALUE	№	WAGES	OFFICE RENT	PETTY CASH	MISC
June 1	Cash	256·56	256	212.80	25.50	18·26	

Total must agree

As on the receipts side, the important rule is that for each cheque issued the total of entries in the analysis columns must be equal to the entry in column 3.

Example

Entries on the payments side for a typical month might be as shown below:

1	2	3	4	5	6	7	8	9	10	11	12	13	14
DATE	PAID TO	CHEQUE VALUE	NO.	MAT-ERIALS	WAGES	OWNERS' DRAW-INGS	SUB CONT-RACTORS	RENT + GEN. EXPS	PLANT RUNNING EXPS	TRANS'P RUNNING EXPS	PLANT HIRE	PETTY CASH	MISC.
June 1	Cash	256.26	236		212.80			25.50				18.26	
June 3	Murungi Bros	129.01					129.01						
June 5	Building Supplies	1216.—		1216.—									
June 8	Cash	321.—			321.—								
June 12	Kisumu Supplies	2046.01		2046.01									
June 15	Cash	309.—			309.—								
June 17	Insurance Services	212.—											212.—
June 20	Murungi Motors	426.—							246.—	180.—			
June 22	Cash	289.—			289.—								
—	H.V. Plant Hire	412.—									412.—		
June 29	Cash	520.—			220.—	300.—							

Other payments and charges

When all the cheque entries for a month have been made, the other payments and charges made directly by the bank must be added. If a concrete mixer or a truck is being bought on hire purchase, the repayments will probably be made by standing order through the bank. This means that the bank is instructed to pay the supplier or finance company a stated sum on the same day of each month for a specified number of months until the debt is repaid. Other items such as half-yearly bank charges will be shown on the bank statement.

Bank statements

Most banks will supply statements of their customer's account whenever they are requested. There will only rarely be mistakes on these but it is still worth checking bank statements to ensure that payments into the account have been correctly credited and that no deductions have been made wrongly which should have been debited to one of the bank's other customers. A typical bank statement sheet might be as illustrated below:

NATIONAL BANK LIMITED

STATEMENT OF ACCOUNT

	DETAIL	PAYMENTS	RECEIPTS	DATE	BALANCE
BALANCE FORWARD				1 June	1054.06
	236	256.26		1 June	797.80
	237	123.01		3 June	674.79
			1076.00	4 June	1750.79
	238	1216.00		5 June	534.79
			4275.00	6 June	4809.79
			821.00	7 June	5630.79
	239	321.00		8 June	5309.79
			67.00	10 June	5376.79
	240	2046.01		12 June	3330.78
			428.00	12 June	3758.78

Check statement from cash analysis book

The bank does not usually show the names written on cheques or the source of receipts in the bank statement. It is sometimes useful to have these on old bank statements for reference purposes, so they should be written in when the statement is checked from the cash analysis book. At that stage any items (bank charges, standing orders, etc.) shown on the statement but not included in cash book entries can be easily identified and written up in the cash book. The bank statement might now look as illustrated below:

NATIONAL BANK LIMITED

STATEMENT OF ACCOUNT

	DETAIL	PAYMENTS	RECEIPTS	DATE	BALANCE
BALANCE FORWARD				1 June	1054.06
Cash (Wages, Rent) (Petty Cash)	236	256.26		1 June	797.80
Murungi Bros.	237	123.01		3 June	674.79
Muringi Motors			1076.00	4 June	1750.79
Building Supplies	238	1216.00		5 June	534.79
Kisumu Council			4275.00	6 June	4809.79
H. Kirby			821.00	7 June	5630.79
Cash (Wages)	239	321.00		8 June	5309.79
Maluki Bros.			67.00	10 June	5376.79
Kisumu Supplies	240	2046.01		12 June	3330.78
Star Hotel			428.00	12 June	3758.78

Checking bank balance

Kaburu Builders' bank statement, illustrated above, shows a positive balance right through the month. Unless a bank has agreed that a client should be permitted to run an overdraft, it will be quite within its rights to refuse to honour cheques which would require more money than is shown in the balance column. If a contractor gets a reputation for issuing cheques which are likely to be dishonoured (or 'bounce'), he will find that suppliers will no longer be prepared to grant credit facilities and his business may be seriously affected. Thus he should keep a running check on his bank balance to ensure that there is no danger of this happening.

Chapter Six
Fixed Assets, Depreciation

Purchase of fixed assets. Assets mean overheads. Recording fixed assets. Going concern assumption. Principle of depreciation. The straight line method. Estimating the life of fixed assets. Examples of depreciation calculations. Checking assumptions on which calculations are based.

Fixed assets

Fixed assets are items like land, buildings, plant, vehicles and equipment which the contractor needs in order to be able to carry out the sort of building activities in which he specialises. They are described as fixed, but this does not mean that they are fixed to the ground. The terms 'fixed assets' and 'fixed capital' mean that money invested in this way will be out of circulation for at least a year.

Current assets

The remaining capital consists of cash and items such as payments due on contract accounts. This is known as current capital and current assets, since this money is available for wage payments and other immediate expenses involved in financing a building contract.

Purchase of fixed assets

One of the most difficult problems which has to be faced by anyone who starts a new business is how much of his funds are to be tied up in the purchase of fixed assets.

Limited initial capital

The problem is made more difficult by the fact that most businesses are started with a limited amount of money. This means that, if too much is expended in purchasing fixed assets to equip the firm properly, the level of current assets may run dangerously low.

Caution in spending on fixed assets

Thus although it is easy to be tempted by glossy advertisements for new plant and machinery, it is vital to remember that current capital needs are always difficult to forecast. If one of the early contracts runs into trouble, the cash flow pattern will be disturbed and extra funds may be needed urgently. Thus caution in spending on fixed assets is often the wisest course.

Example: New Construction Company Limited

To show some of the factors that may have to be considered in coming to a decision, we will invent a new firm and see how the owners tackle the problem.

Let us start at the moment when two men decide to go into business as building contractors. They first form a company which we shall call the 'New Construction Partnership'

Experience

Let us suppose that one of the partners has a considerable practical experience of building, having been for some years a site foreman for a large contracting firm. He has managed to save a certain amount of money, say $2000, which he is prepared to put into the business.

Money

The other partner is a more wealthy trader with considerable experience of business and commerce, but who has little technical knowledge of the building industry. He is prepared to invest $8,000 in this activity.

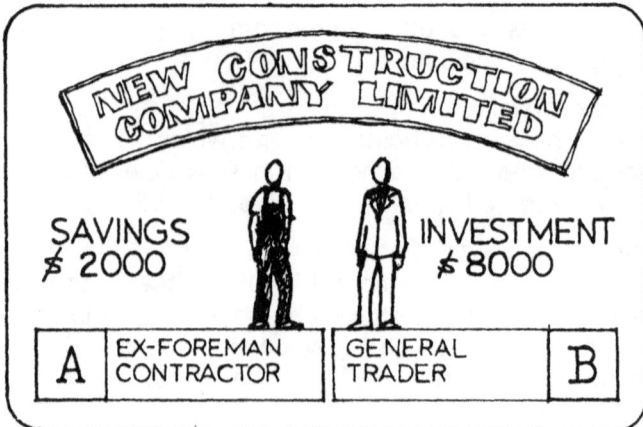

A good partnership

This is at least a partnership which seems to stand some chance of success. One man brings technical experience and a little capital. The other brings money as well as financial and commercial expertise. It is surprising how often men go into business with partners who do not add to their own abilities or experience.

Bad partnership

Let us suppose the foreman had started a business with another foreman. They might be great friends and very hard working — but they would both lack trading and business experience — and equally important they would start without enough capital.

Equally the trader might have gone into business with a colleague. With their combined resources their business would have plenty of capital. But what would happen when they started to trade?

They would have to employ a manager and trust him completely, for in technical matters he could tell them that materials had to be brought from a certain merchant at a high price. They would not know that the price was too high and that the foreman was collecting a bribe from the merchant!

Complementary skills

Thus the wise man will take a partner who **adds** to his experience rather than duplicates it.

Purchase of fixed assets

For simplicity we will assume that fixed assets are purchased before the company starts to trade. In real life, of course, the company will probably start to trade before investing in buildings and plant.

How much on fixed assets?

Let us suppose, however, that the New Construction Company has a firm promise of several contracts.

Thus the directors must consider how much money can be allotted for the purchase of fixed assets.

Leave enough for current assets

This decision should be based on a budget, or forecast of the firm's financial needs. It is vital that enough money should be left as current assets to finance the contracts through their difficult early stages, leaving an additional safety factor to cope with difficulties that cannot be foreseen.

Half and half

Our two directors, after careful thought, decide that the capital sum can be split evenly between fixed and current assets and $5,000 can safely be allocated for the purchase of fixed assets.

Assets mean overheads

The next stage is to list the essentials that they will need to carry on their business. They have to remember that assets give rise to overheads, and overheads have to be recovered as an addition to direct costs before any activity can show a profit.

After further discussion they decide that they will need a small building as an office and store. There will obviously be a need to buy various small tools, such as wheelbarrows and shovels. A pick-up truck will be necessary to transport tools and materials. They also decide it would be wise to keep some money back as plant reserves, in case they need to buy specialist tools or plant for any additional contracts that might be obtained in the first year.

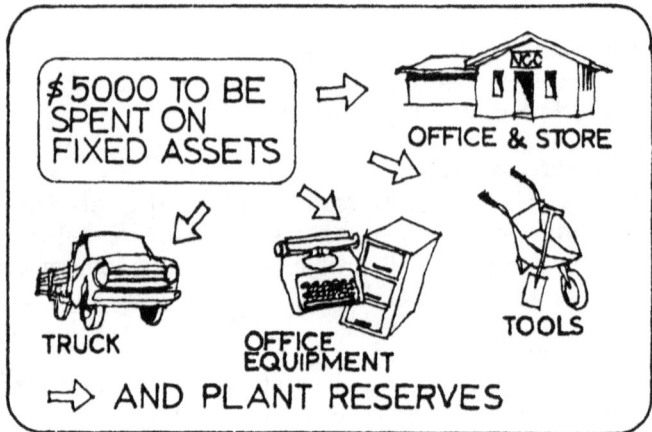

An office

First they must seek suitable premises, ideally an office with a piece of land attached on which plant and materials can be stored.

They enquire among their friends and read the newspaper advertisements and eventually hear of a piece of land for sale with a small building on it. They visit the owner, and after a long negotiation, obtain it for $2,000. The building is big

96

enough to act as both office and stores — so no further work on the building will be necessary at this stage.

Office equipment

An office is no use without equipment and $200 is set aside for a desk, a chair, filing cabinet and other office equipment.

Tools

$800 goes to buy tools and plant including a small concrete mixer.

Truck

They also need a small pick-up truck to carry tools and materials between contracts and, to avoid hiring costs, they buy a second hand one at a cost of $1,200.

Plant reserves

This leaves $800 for plant reserves, which can be used to buy specialist tools for any other contracts that might be obtained in the first year.

Fixed assets

So the total of fixed assets is as follows:

FIXED ASSETS

LAND AND BUILDINGS	2000
OFFICE EQUIPMENT	200
PLANT AND TOOLS	800
MOTOR VEHICLES	1200
PLANT RESERVES	800
	$ 5000

Current assets

This leaves $5,000 for current assets which will pay wages, materials, hire of plant and incidental expenses on jobs until payments are received from the client. The directors will have to bear this sum in mind as they tender for work and ensure that the jobs which they take on will not require finance in excess of this sum.

CURRENT ASSETS

FOR: WAGES
     MATERIALS   } UNTIL PAYMENT
     PLANT HIRE   } RECEIVED
     INCIDENTAL   } FROM CLIENT
       EXPENSES   }

ORIGINAL CASH	$ 10,000
FIXED ASSETS	5,000
LEAVES FOR CURRENT ASSETS	$ 5,000

Recording fixed assets

When any item which could come under the heading of fixed assets is purchased, it is recorded in the books at its cost value. The cost figure shown should include all costs of acquisition and making it ready for use. In purchasing buildings, the legal cost of transferring land and surveyor's fees should be included. If a block-making machine is purchased, costs of providing a concrete foundation should be included in the fixed cost, even if the work is carried out by the contractor's own labour force.

Valuation of current assets

The valuation of assets always presents a tricky problem. Even current assets such as 'work in progress', 'materials on site' or 'debtors' can only be estimated, based on certain assumptions. Unexpected construction faults, stock losses due to theft or bad debts could all lead to errors.

PROBLEMS IN VALUING CURRENT ASSETS

WORK IN ——— MATERIALS ——— DEBTORS
PROGRESS   ON SITE

Should turn back into cash

At least errors in current assets show themselves fairly quickly, because they are by definition expected to turn back into cash fairly quickly. If this fails to occur, there is a clear indication that something has gone wrong.

Fixed assets more difficult

Errors in fixed assets can be more serious, since they are expected to last for a number of years and so discrepancies are less obvious. If the accountant is ever going to hope to have some systematic way of measuring the financial progress of a business, it is obvious that some assumptions are going to have to be made.

The question of value

To start with, there is the question of what is true value. Let us start with the second hand pick-up truck bought by the New Construction Company. We know that they paid $1,200 for it. What we cannot know accurately is its market value the following day. If they visited six dealers, they might be offered six different prices ranging from $800 to $1,100. It is even possible that some private individual would feel that $1,200 was less than its real value and might make an offer of $1,250. If they tested the market the following week, a whole new series of quotations might be offered.

Problems of regular revaluation

The whole question of accurate revaluation of fixed assets on a regular basis is clearly so complicated and contentious that it would be wise for us to seize on any definite figure that is available and use that as a basis for calculation.

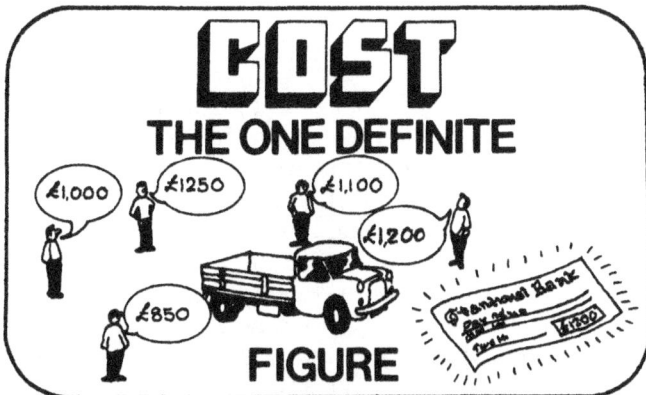

Cost

The one clear and unarguable figure relating to the pick-up truck is that it cost $1,200. The great advantage of that figure is that it is not an informed guess by a valuer, but represents an actual transaction between a willing buyer and a willing seller. It is shown in the cash analysis book, and the evidence of the transaction is the cheque for $1,200 paid to the motor dealer.

Adjusting cost figures

It will be necessary to adjust cost figures for fixed assets to take account of the fact that most forms of fixed assets gradually wear out and lose their value. This is done by making allowances for 'depreciation', which will be discussed later. However at least we now have an objective way to value assets, which can be substantiated by facts and figures and can be understood by anyone who comes to look at the accounts.

One more assumption

There is one more assumption that is normally made by accountants which should be mentioned at this stage, since it affects both current and fixed assets.

An example

To understand the reasoning behind this assumption let us suppose that we are valuing our personal possessions. We come to value our personal clothing, which to us is a fixed asset since we use it in our daily lives and expect it to last for a reasonable time. We know that no two persons would put the same valuation on it, so we have decided to base our calculations on its cost with some adjustment to take account of wear and tear.

Value to us

The important thing is that our adjusted price should give a realistic estimate of the value of the clothing to *us*. It is not necessarily the sort of sum that would be offered to us if we had to sell it. If my suit cost $100 and I estimate $40 for wear and tear, then I can be quite confident in showing $60 for the suit, since I intend to go on wearing it for quite a while and, even if I did sell it, I would have to find considerably more money than $60 to buy a new one of similar quality. The fact that I would only be offered $10 for it in the market just does not matter at all.

Changing circumstances

But suppose circumstances were to change. If I were to move to a country with a different climate, or perhaps even to die, the clothing would no longer be of any use to me and would have to be sold. This would mean that the valuation based upon adjusted original cost would no longer be valid.

Assume continue in business

So in fact my valuation of $60 for my suit is based on the assumption that I am going to continue with my present life style for long enough to wear it out. In the same way we value the pick-up truck owned by the New Construction Company on the basis that it will continue in business as a going concern.

Going concern assumption

This assumption that any particular business will continue as a going concern is a further fundamental principle of accounting. This assumption is vital in assessing current assets as well as fixed assets. For example, we value 'work in progress' on sites on the assumption that the work will be completed in accordance with the contract. If this were not to hold good, the contractor would have to pay liquidated damages which would probably be greater than the value of 'work in progress'.

ASSUME BUSINESS

NEW CONSTRUCTION COMPANY

IS A GOING CONCERN

Two assumptions

Without these two assumptions that:

1. Valuation of assets is based on *cost*;
2. The business will continue as a going concern;

it would not be possible to produce accounts on an objective basis that would allow the financial performance of a firm to be measured and compared from year to year. However, we will have to remember that the assumptions have been made if we are considering buying an existing business.

Buying a business: Caution

It will be useful to know that the net assets in the balance sheet are shown at, say, $19,486.23. But this does not mean that we should pay exactly that sum. It will be necessary to look carefully at all the individual assets as well as the prospects for continuing and expanding the business before we decide what sort of financial offer would be justified.

Adjusting cost figures

We have decided to base the figure on which we show fixed assets in the balance sheet upon their cost, since these are definite figures justified by actual financial transactions. But we have also recognised that most forms of fixed asset gradually wear out, so the cost figure will have to be adjusted regularly if successive balance sheets are to be reasonably realistic.

Depreciation

The term used for the reduction in the original cost of fixed assets to take account of wear and tear is depreciation. It is obvious that different assets will depreciate at different rates. No asset, apart from land, can last for ever. But some, like buildings, may last for 50 to 100 years, so they will lose their original cost value only very slowly. Other items, like vehicles and mechanical plant, can be expected to wear out much more quickly.

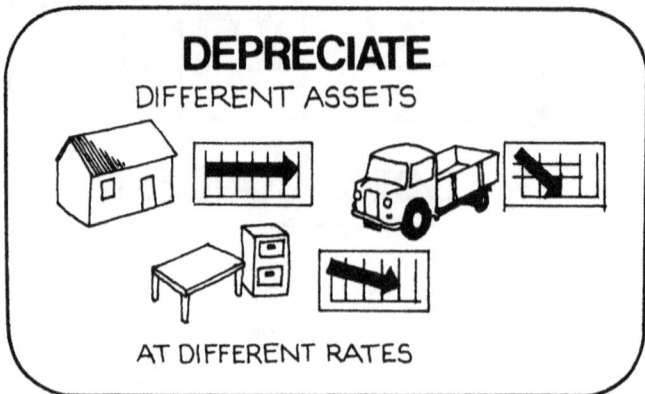

DEPRECIATE
DIFFERENT ASSETS

AT DIFFERENT RATES

Reserves

We have said that we assume, unless there is evidence to the contrary, that a firm is a going concern and that it is going to continue to trade well into the future. It can only hope to do this if its plant, equipment and other assets are kept up to date. Depreciation allows this to happen by ensuring that a proportion of the original cost of each asset is written off each year. This money can be placed in some kind of reserve fund to ensure that when, for example, a concrete mixer reaches the end of its useful life there is money available to buy a new one.

Two reasons

An asset can become useless for one of two reasons. First, it might simply wear out physically. Second, new developments of more modern and suitable equipment may make the existing equipment obsolete. Either way, after a given number of years, money will be needed to replace it.

Example: Private motor car

An everyday example of an asset which gradually loses value is a private motor car. If we buy a motor car, we try to buy one that will last as long as possible and keep it properly serviced and repaired. But even so, after about ten years its trade-in value will be next to nothing. Suppose a particular motor car is bought in 1977 for $4,000 and a fair guess at its life is ten years.

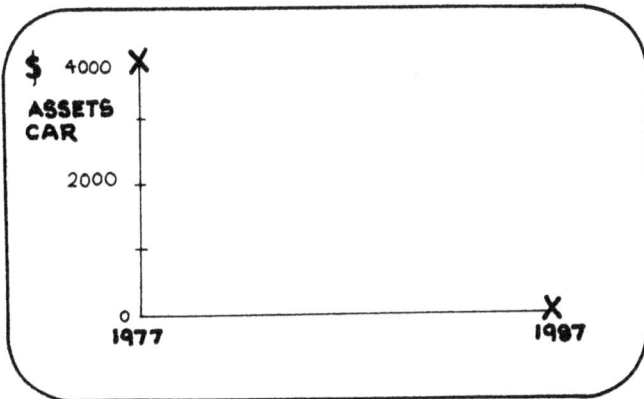

Two facts

Now we have two 'facts', which can be used in our accounting calculations. If we draw up a personal Balance Sheet for

1977 we would show among our assets a motor car at $4,000. If we draw up an estimate of a personal Balance Sheet for 1987 the motor car will not appear because it has a nil estimated value. If we were to draw up a chart to show the value in each year, we would now have two definite points each marked by a cross as illustrated on the previous page.

Need to save $4,000

Thus over the ten years we will have to save up a total $4,000 out of our salary or wages if our personal accounts in 1987 are to show a similar asset value to that in 1977. This sum of $4,000 must be divided up in some way so that a part is shown as an expense against income each year.

Changing asset into expense

Since accounting assumes that some portion of an asset is used up during each year of its life, we have to decide on some way of estimating what portion should be treated as an expense in any given year. So depreciation is actually a way of changing an asset into a series of annual expenses. At the end of the asset's life, the total of the annual expenses is equal to the original cost of the asset.

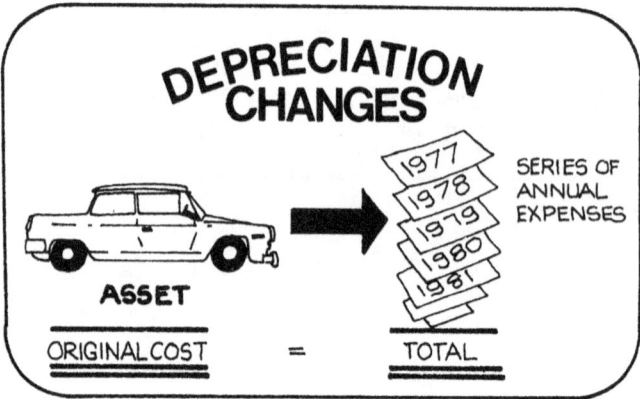

Many methods

There are many methods of calculating depreciation and the method chosen will affect the annual net profit figure for the years in question.

Two extremes

For example, we could assume that all our $4,000 depreciation occurred in 1977, but that would not be realistic because it would look as though we were incompetent and made a big loss in 1977 when in fact it might have been quite a good year. At the other extreme we could charge little or no depreciation in the first nine years and leave it all until 1987. But this would also be unrealistic, because our balance sheet asset figure would be overstated for nine years and the profits figure would look better than it really was. These two extremes are shown as Route One and Route Two on the chart below:

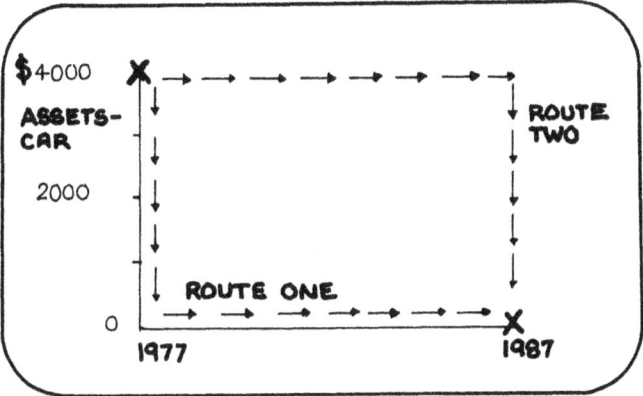

Choosing a line

Since the two extremes are both clearly unrealistic we must choose a way to draw a line to connect the two crosses that lies somewhere in the rectangle between Route One and Route Two.

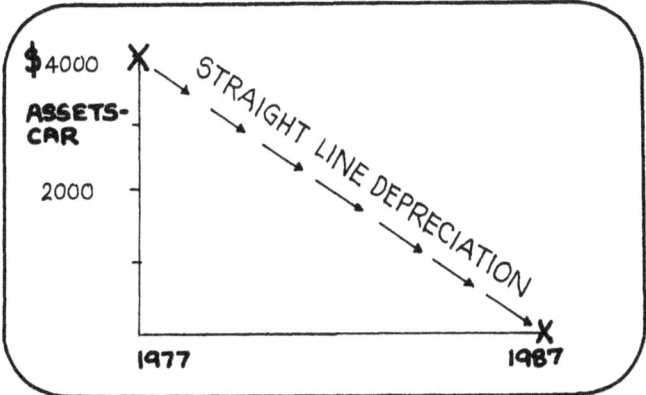

The straight line method

One simple way would be to take an exact middle course and draw a straight line between the two. This would mean

105

that we assume that the asset loses its initial value at a constant rate over the whole of its life. This is a quite reasonable assumption in many cases, and this common way of calculating depreciation is known as the straight-line method of depreciation.

Easy to calculate

A great advantage of the straight line method of calculating depreciation is that it is very easy to calculate. It is not even necessary to draw up a chart in every case. All that the accountant has to do is estimate the life of each asset in years and divide the number of years into the cost of the asset to find the depreciation. This depreciation is then charged as an expense in the profit and loss account for each year of the life of asset.

CALCULATING **STRAIGHT LINE** DEPRECIATION

$$\left(\frac{\text{COST OF ASSET}}{\text{ESTIMATED LIFE}}\right) = \text{ANNUAL DEPRECIATION}$$

New Construction Company

Going back to the New Construction Company Limited, we can now estimate the life of the various assets and calculate annual depreciation.

FIXED ASSETS

LAND AND BUILDINGS	2000
OFFICE EQUIPMENT	200
PLANT AND TOOLS	800
MOTOR VEHICLES	1200
PLANT RESERVES	800
	$ 5000

Pick-up truck

Starting with the pick-up truck which cost $1,200, we will assume a life of six years. This means that $200 depreciation will have to be allowed for each year, and the depreciation chart will be as illustrated below:

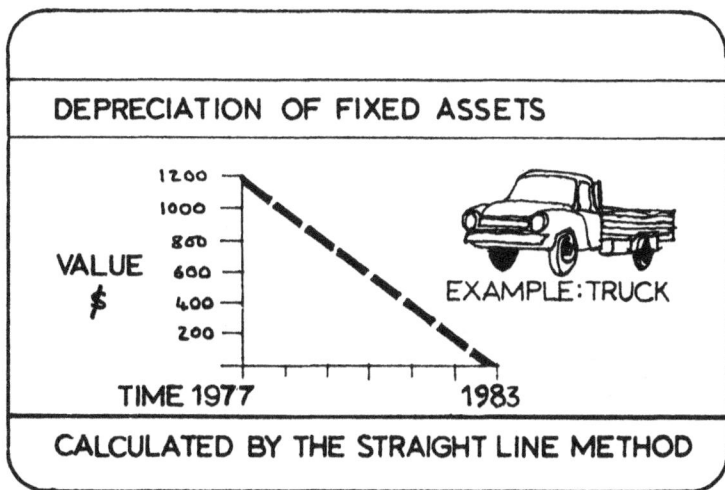

DEPRECIATION OF FIXED ASSETS

VALUE $

1200
1000
800
600
400
200

EXAMPLE: TRUCK

TIME 1977   1983

CALCULATED BY THE STRAIGHT LINE METHOD

Land and buildings

Land normally does not depreciate. In fact it can increase in value quite sharply in inflationary times. Buildings however will eventually have to be replaced, so we will assume that the partners estimate the life of land and buildings as 50 years. The cost was $2,000, so $40 depreciation should be allowed each year.

Office equipment

Office equipment includes a number of items with different lives. However, a fair average life might be ten years, so the cost of $200 could be written off using an annual depreciation of $20.

Plant and equipment

Plant and equipment also includes a number of separate items. For present purposes, we will assume an average life of eight years. Thus the cost of $800 will be written off by the straight line method using an annual depreciation of $100.

Plant reserves

The sum of $800 cash was retained for future purchases. This cash is not assumed by accountants to depreciate, since inflation is neglected in conventional accounting procedures. Thus the plant reserves will not attract depreciation until they are actually spent on physical assets of some kind.

Calculating depreciation

It is convenient to calculate depreciation by listing assets, with columns for cost, life and depreciation as illustrated below:

DEPRECIATION			
ASSET	Initial Value	Life in Years	Write off Each Yr.
	(1)	(2)	(3)
Land & Buildings	2000	50	40
Office Equipment	200	10	20
Plant & Equipment	800	8	100
Motor Vehicles	1200	6	200
Plant Reserves (not used)	800	- -	- -
			360

The depreciation on each item is given in Column 3 by dividing Column 1 by Column 2. The total depreciation should result in sufficient money being saved each year to maintain the balance sheet value of assets in a realistic way. In this particular case the figure is $360.

How soon to write off?

We have made certain estimates of the life of the assets of the New Construction Company Limited. In real life decisions on these estimates are very difficult to make, and errors can be quite serious in the way they distort a firm's accounts. But estimates have to be made, because at the time an item of equipment is purchased there is no way of knowing for certain how long it will last. All that can be done is to give an honest estimate on the basis of a reasonable standard of knowledge and experience.

Example: Concrete mixer

To show the way in which different estimates of the life of an asset can affect reported profits, we will consider the simple example of two plant hire firms. Let us assume that they are equally efficient. They each buy identical makes of concrete mixer for $300 and are both able to generate an annual operating profit, after running costs but before depreciation, of $150.

Company X and Company Y

We will call the two firms Company X and Company Y. There is no difference between them in real life, and they can be seen as identical twins. We will see, however, that different accounting assumptions can give a very different picture of them, although the assumptions made are in neither case unreasonable.

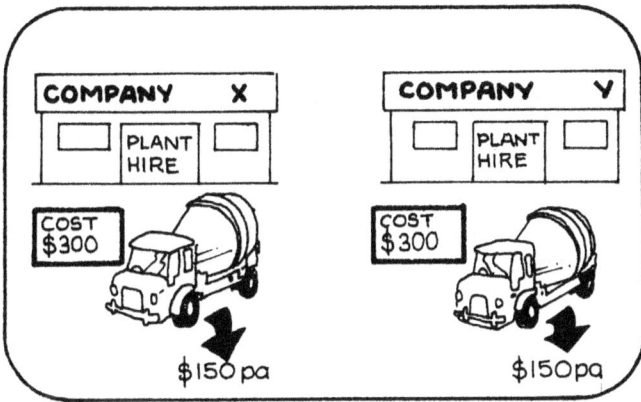

Company X — three years

The only difference between the two firms, Company X and Company Y, is the estimate of the useful life of the concrete mixer. The directors of Company X estimate that it has a life of three years, so the first year's profit is:

$$\$150 - \frac{(300)}{(3)}$$
$$= \$150 - 100 = \$50$$

Company Y — five years

But the directors of Company Y are more optimistic. They estimate that their (identical) mixer will last two years longer, so their first year's profit is:

$$\$150 - \frac{(300)}{(5)}$$
$$= \$150 - 60 = \$90$$

109

Higher profit shown

Thus we have two companies which are equally efficient, but one showing a profit 80% higher than the other.

This is an important point to remember if you are considering buying a business. Always check that the profits in real life are the same as those shown on paper.

Comparative value

To see this effect suppose we were valuing the companies at the end of the third year. The figures would be as follows:

	Co. X	Co. Y
Fixed Assets	Nil	$120
Profit Year 1	$50	90
2	50	90
3	50	90
(Plant reserves)	(300)	(180)

VALUATION AT END OF YEAR 3:		
	COMPANY X	COMPANY Y
FIXED ASSETS	NIL	$ 120
PROFIT YEAR 1	$ 50	90
2	50	90
3	50	90
(PLANT RESERVES)	(300)	(180)

Good appearance of Y

We know that the two companies are equally efficient. But the accounts tell a different story. Company Y appears to be the only one with profit-earning assets, and for the last three years its owners have been able to take out $90 in profits each year.

But X the better firm

But the fact is that Company X is the better firm for, not only does it own a mixer in just as good condition as the other, but it already possesses enough capital to buy a second mixer.

Fourth year

In the fourth year Company Y will only be able to show a profit of $90. But Company X will show a profit of $150 on its first mixer (no depreciation) and $50 on its second mixer, making a total of $200. (We can note that the three-year old mixer shows three times the profit of a new one in this instance — another example of the way figures can mislead.)

Fifth year

By the end of the fifth year the paper figures will be:

VALUATION AT END OF YEAR 5		
	COMPANY X	COMPANY Y
FIXED ASSETS	$ 100	NIL
PROFIT YEAR 1	50	$ 90
2	50	90
3	50	90
4	200	90
5	200	90
(PLANT RESERVES)	(200)	(300)

X looks better now

Now Company X looks by far the better buy, with a record of increasing profits while Company Y has no profit-earning assets at all.

Must understand

A shrewd trader might well have convinced a buyer who didn't understand how to deal with figures that in year three he should sell Company X and buy Company Y. This is the reason we say that a manager who cannot deal with figures is like a carpenter who cannot use a saw!

Object of the story

The object of telling this story is not to suggest that accounts do not have much meaning. It is to suggest that it is always wise to check the basis for the calculations and the sort of assumptions which have been made. Depreciation is a valuable tool of the accountant's trade, which allows accounts to be much more realistic than if all assets were written off as costs in the year in which they were acquired. But, like all tools of the builders trade, it can be dangerous in the hands of anyone who does not know how to use it properly.

Chapter Seven

Balance Sheets

Balance sheet as a 'snapshot' of a business. Function of the balance sheet. Goodwill. Owners' capital. Typical balance sheet. Measuring work in progress. Debtors and creditors. Investments. Horizontal and vertical forms of presentation of a balance sheet. The trial balance. Transfer of balancing figures. Common book-keeping mistakes. Checking with analysis book method.

Factors and skills

There are many different factors and skills that are needed if a contractor is to prove successful in his business life. He must be able to estimate and tender, to plan the best way to carry out the work, to organise his labour force, to deal quickly and effectively with problems as they arise and ensure that contracts are completed on time and to standards of quality that are acceptable to clients and customers.

Financial health

With all these tasks to cope with, it is necessary to be able occasionally to check up on the financial health of the business to make sure that all the efforts put in by the contractor and his staff are making the business stronger and increasing its resources.

Not always as they seem

The position has to be calculated because things are not always really as they might seem from a personal impression. A firm might have plenty of money in the bank because it is slow to pay its creditors, but really be making a loss. On the other hand it might be completing contracts in record time and at good profit margins, but clients may be so slow to pay that debtors reach alarming proportions and cash flow suffers accordingly. If depreciation is not properly allowed for, paper profits may look good for several years until the time comes to replace major items of plant.

Count up

With all these possibilities, the wise contractor regularly has a 'count up' to find out what his business is really worth and whether he is making a reasonable profit. This can only be done by taking stock of every part of the business shown in the accounts: creditors, debtors, work in progress, loans, owners' capital, fixed and current assets.

At least once a year

In the case of a limited company, the directors are required by law to have this 'count up' at least once a year, and provide a balance sheet and profit and loss account audited by an independent accountant. In fact most businesses need to provide this sort of information annually for taxation purposes, and it will also be necessary if there is any intention of seeking a loan from the bank or perhaps even if extended credit is to be sought from a supplier.

Possibly more frequent

Of course it may well be worthwhile to produce figures in this form more frequently for internal management use to check on the progress of the business, although these interim figures would not normally be reviewed by an outside auditor.

Statement

The balance sheet is not merely another account, although it is prepared from the figures shown in the account books of a business. The balance sheet is in fact a statement of the financial standing of a business as reflected by its:

1. Assets   2. Liabilities   3. Owners' capital.

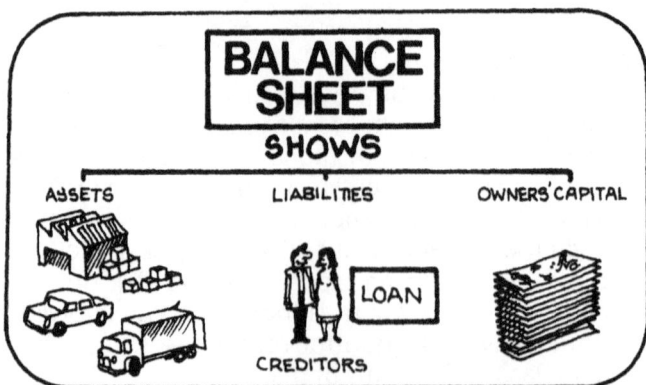

Constant change

We know that businesses are constantly changing, so a balance sheet can only give a correct picture of the financial standing of a business on one particular day. We could see the accountant as a photographer and the balance sheet as a 'snapshot' of the business. The camera could be likened to the accounting procedures that have to be undertaken in order to produce the balance sheet or statement.

The remainder of this chapter is intended to give an introduction to these accounting procedures.

BALANCE SHEET IS A SNAPSHOT OF THE BUSINESS

ACCOUNTANT

New transactions

Even on the day after the balance sheet date, the picture will start to change as new transactions are undertaken. A cheque may be received from a client and be paid into the bank, increasing 'cash at bank' and reducing 'debtors'. Materials may be delivered to one of the sites, wage and salary payments may be made or a new concrete mixer purchased.

Strengths and weaknesses

Although the figures start to get out of date the day after the balance sheet date, this does not mean that it ceases to have a useful story to tell. If the balance sheet has been prepared carefully and honestly, it will give a clear and accurate picture of the strengths and weaknesses of the firm.

Understanding balance sheets

Of course the picture can only be accurately read and properly understood by someone who understands a certain amount about accounting, just as the working drawings of a building can only be properly understood by someone who understands a certain amount about building. Since the contractor is a businessman as well as a builder, he needs both of these skills. Even if he does not reach the stage of being able to produce a balance sheet himself, he should be capable of understanding how it is put together and what it can show (as well as what it cannot show!) about the state of his business.

Function of balance sheet

It is the function of a balance sheet to show how money has been used, what sort of assets it has been turned into and how much of the assets belong to the owners and any other people who have a claim on the business.

Three headings

To start with the figures in the balance sheet have to be grouped under the three main headings:

1. Assets
2. Liabilities
3. Owner's investment.

Assets

The assets could also be seen as the financial resources of the business. Total assets include both fixed assets (such as buildings, plant and vehicles) and current assets (such as stock, debtors, cash, etc.). Current assets change from day to day. Fixed assets also change, but more rarely as they depreciate, are sold or supplemented by new purchases.

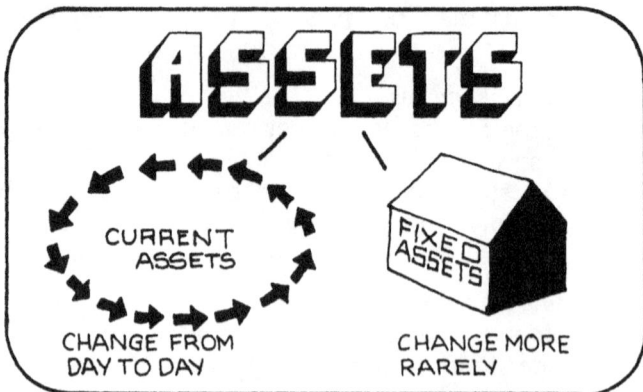

ASSETS

CURRENT ASSETS

FIXED ASSETS

CHANGE FROM DAY TO DAY

CHANGE MORE RARELY

Goodwill

One sometimes sees an item under assets labelled 'goodwill'. Of course all good, profitable and effective businesses enjoy the goodwill of their clients in the sense that they are respected as capable and honest in their dealings. Indeed some of the most important qualities, such as a skilled, loyal and well-trained labour force cannot be accurately valued in cash terms. But 'goodwill' in accounting terminology results when an existing business is bought by new owners. If the new owners pay more than the value shown for assets in the balance sheet, the excess payment is termed 'goodwill' and can be shown in the new owners' balance sheet under that heading.

Intangible assets

Goodwill is an intangible asset, since it is not represented by cash, agreed debts or any solid item which can be objectively valued as an entity. The existence of intangible assets makes balance sheets less easy to compare, so it is standard practice to write off goodwill as soon as possible. This does not mean that it is not worthwhile for a contractor to build his reputation for integrity and good work, but simply that it is hard to put a valid cash sum on it for accounting purposes.

Liabilities

The liabilities shown in the balance sheet of a firm on a particular date represent the obligations of that firm to pay money to outsiders for various purposes. Some of these liabilities may be long term if a debenture or loan has been raised which will not have to be repaid for several years. Other liabilities are current including creditors, current taxation, wages and salaries, etc.

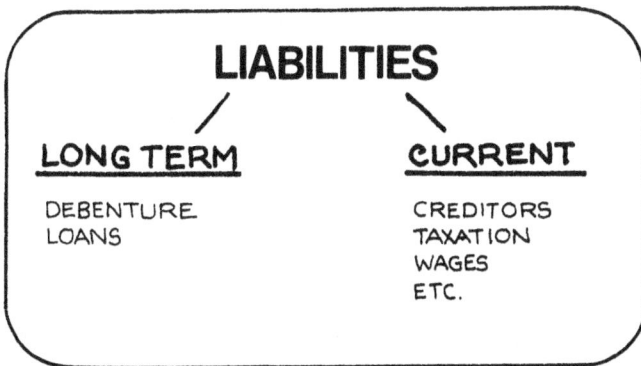

LIABILITIES

LONG TERM

DEBENTURE
LOANS

CURRENT

CREDITORS
TAXATION
WAGES
ETC.

Assets should exceed liabilities

Assuming that the firm is solvent, total assets must be greater than liabilities. If this is not the case, the firm is in no position to meet its debts and should stop trading or be placed in the hands of a liquidator or receiver. The liquidator or receiver would take over the management of the business from the previous owners (whose investment is by now worthless) and attempt to realise sufficient funds to repay as much as possible to the creditors.

Owners' capital

If assets do exceed liabilities, the difference between the two belongs to the owners of the firm and is called 'owners' capital'. This will consist of the money that the owners put into the business in the first place, together with other funds or reserves that have been left over from profits earned over the years but not taken out in the form of dividends or drawings.

Balance

The most common way of drawing up a balance sheet is to show owners' capital and liabilities on the left and assets on the right. Since owners' capital is the difference between assets and liabilities, the totals on the left and the right should 'balance' or be exactly the same.

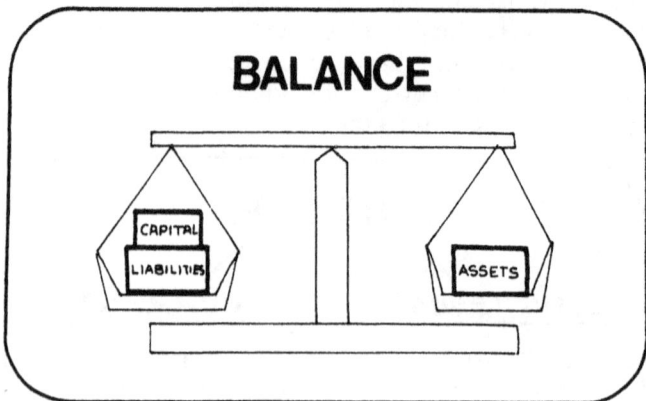

Typical balance sheet

Before we examine the ways in which various figures are brought together and organised into the three 'parcels of money' that make up a balance sheet, we can take a look at a typical balance sheet and the meaning of the various elements which it contains:

Typical Balance Sheet				
As at 31st March 1978				
Owners' Capital	$	*Fixed Assets*		$
Issued capital	10,000	Land and buildings	6,800	
($1 ordinary shares)		(at cost 1972)		
Balance on profit and		Plant and		
loss account	19,700	machinery 8,100		
		Less		
		Depreciation 5,200	2,900	9,700
	29,700			
Current Liabilities		*Current Assets*		
Creditors 2,300		Work in progress	7,500	
Taxation 600	2,900	Debtors	5,000	
		Cash at bank/in hand	4,000	
		Investments (market		
		value $10,000)	6,400	22,900
	32,600			32,600

Balance sheet does balance

The first thing to check is that the balance sheet does in fact balance. The total of owners' capital ($29,700) and liabilities ($2,900) is $32,600 and the total assets add up to the same figure of $32,600.

Owners' capital

The owners appear to have put up $10,000 to get the company started. Happily the company has been profitable, and they have not spent all the profits immediately on their personal needs but have left a total of $19,700 in the firm. This means that each $1 share is now more valuable and is backed by $2.97 of assets.

Current liabilities

In this case there are no fixed liabilities. The current liabilities consist of 'Creditors' and 'Taxation'. The figure of

$2,300 owing to creditors is probably not just one sum of money owing to a particular materials merchant, but a total figure resulting from the addition of amounts owing on quite a number of individual small accounts.

Fixed assets

The assets are shown on the right hand side of the balance sheet, and it is standard practice to divide them into fixed assets and current assets. It will be noticed that land and buildings are shown at cost, without depreciation in this particular case. The cost of plant and machinery is also shown under fixed assets, but depreciation has been deducted so that the balance sheet figure is reasonably realistic.

Current assets

The current assets for this particular firm on this particular date come under four headings:

1. Work in progress
2. Debtors
3. Cash at bank/cash in hand
4. Investments.

Work in progress

Work in progress consists of work that has been carried out on behalf of clients, but for which they have not yet been billed. For example work to the value of $12,500 may have been carried out on a school contract on the balance sheet date, but the settlement of the last interim certificate may have brought payments from the client to a total of $10,000. The extra sum of $2,500 represents real costs of resources such as labour, plant and materials, so the balance sheet would not give an accurate picture if it was ignored.

Materials on site

Within the overall figure for work in progress there will probably be a figure which represents the value of materials on the site but not yet incorporated in the construction work. These must also be allowed for in the balance sheet since they will have gone into the contractor's books as a transaction when they were received. Even if they have not yet been paid for the cost of these materials will have been included as a debit item under 'Creditors' so it is right that they should also appear on the other side of the balance sheet.

120

Measuring work in progress

There is no short cut to calculating the value of work in progress. It is necessary to measure the value of uncertified work on each site on the date of the balance sheet, and then add all these figures together to get a total for the firm as a whole.

Estimate 'as at' balance sheet date

If it is not possible to do this on the particular day that the balance sheet refers to, say the 31st March, then the value of work must be measured on the closest date and an estimate made of the value on 31st March. Thus it is common practice to put the date on the top of the balance sheet 'as at the 31st March' to show that some of the figures it contains are estimates of costs and values at that date rather than direct measurements.

Debtors

The figure for debtors is reasonably easy to calculate in most contracting businesses. There are usually not very many contracts underway at any one time, so it is simply a matter of getting a total of amounts owing on existing and past contracts. It is a little more complicated for the jobbing builder who carries out a large number of small maintenance and renovation jobs but, providing his accounting records have been kept methodically, there should be no difficulty in reaching an accurate total.

Cash in hand

For most contractors, the cash in hand will not be a large figure. There may be an office petty cash float, and possibly other floats for site foremen to make local purchases.

Cash at bank

Assuming that the contractor only operates a single current account, the cash at bank will be available from the bank statement. It may be necessary to adjust the credit balance figure shown by the client to include cheques or amounts paid in that relate to debtors or creditors shown elsewhere. Again the figure will be 'as at' the balance sheet date, rather than the figure actually shown against that date on the bank statement.

Investments

The typical balance sheet shows a figure of $6,400 for investments. Investments represent part ownership of other enterprises, or perhaps result from the investment of surplus cash in government securities. One example might be a contractor putting up some capital to help a carpenter set up in business to make doors, window frames, etc. Besides hoping for dividends from a share in the prospective profits, the contractor might hope to benefit from a good source of timber products for his building activities.

Market value in brackets

It is customary to show the investment in the balance sheet at its cost figure, or the market value if that is lower. However, where the cost figure is used the market value should also be shown in brackets.

Comparative figures

The balance sheet we have just examined was prepared as at a certain date. Balance sheets are normally required to show comparative figures for the previous accounting period, usually the previous year. This allows the reader to see any changes in the stability of the business, and to study trends in the various sub-heads of the statement. The usual practice is to show the current figures on the right of their description and the previous figures on the left.

Horizontal form of balance sheet

This example showed a balance sheet presented in horizontal form, with assets on the right hand side and liabilities on the left hand side. It has the advantage of showing clearly the balance between assets and liabilities.

Vertical form

Balance sheets can, however, also be presented in a vertical form as indicated in the next illustration.

Management purposes

The vertical form of presentation is sometimes more convenient for management purposes, since it is possible to compare the figures for several previous accounting periods by adding additional columns. This is often helpful to outsiders who are considering whether to have dealings with it, such as a bank manager considering whether to offer overdraft facilities. In addition a comparison between current assets and current liabilities, which gives a measure of the liquidity of the business, is rather easier with the vertical form of presentation.

122

Typical Balance Sheet

As at 31st March 1978

			$
Work in progress	7,500		
Debtors	5,000		
Cash at bank/in hand	4,000		
Investments (market value $10,000)	6,400		
			22,900
Less Current Liabilities			
Creditors	2,300		
Taxation	600		2,900
Net Current Assets			20,000
Fixed Assets			
Land and building (at cost 1972)		6,800	
Plant and machinery	8,100		
Less Depreciation	5,200	2,900	9,700
			29,700

Represented by:	
Issued Capital	
10,000 Ordinary Shares of $1	10,000
Balance on Profit and Loss Account	19,700
	29,700

Drawing up final accounts

The balance sheet and the profit and loss account are known as the final accounts. The profit and loss account is a genuine account, and records the effect of the transactions entered into by a business during a specified period. In fact the profit and loss account can be seen as bridging the gap between one balance sheet date and the next, as it describes the changes that have taken place and helps to explain differences between them.

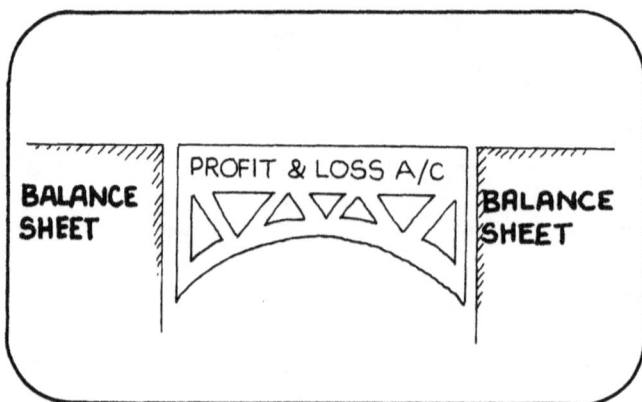

Affect each other

Although the balance sheet is different in many ways from the profit and loss account, they affect each other and the figures used to prepare the profit and loss account react on those in the balance sheet and vice-versa.

Trial balance

The first stage in turning all the separate accounts which must be used in double-entry book-keeping into final accounts is the taking of a trial balance.

A trial balance is a list of balances on either the debit or credit side of all the accounts in the ledger including cash and bank balances.

Totals of debits and credits should be equal

We know that the basic principle of double-entry book-keeping is that every transaction that is recorded must have a credit entry in one place and an equal and opposite debit entry somewhere else. That means that at every stage in the recording of transactions the total of the debit and credit entries resulting from postings from the journal, the sales day book, the purchases day book, the cash book and other subsidiary books should be equal.

Mistakes can be made

But book-keeping is a complicated process which demands an eye for detail and a painstaking approach. Unfortunately book-keepers, like other people, are not perfect and can make mistakes. Thus one reason for making a trial balance is to see whether the total debit and credit items are in fact equal. The trial balance is really a trial of the book-keeper's skill, and if it shows that a mistake has been made he will have to work back through the ledger accounts to correct it.

Typical trial balance

A typical trial balance is in the form shown in the following illustration:

TRIAL BALANCE As at 31st March 1978			
No.	NAME	Dr.	Cr.
1	Capital A/c		2,200
2	Purchases A/c	4,100	
3	Office Expenses A/c	805	
4	Wages A/c	760	
5	Sales A/c		4,500
6	Motor Vehicles A/c	505	
7	Cash at Bank	1,800	
8	Cash in hand	100	
9	Sundry debtors	2,000	
10	Sundry creditors		3,370
		10,070	10,070

Looks like journal page

At first sight, the trial balance looks like a page from the journal. In fact a sheet ruled for a journal page can be used quite conveniently for a trial balance.

No date column

There are several differences however. First we see that the date column has been changed. This is because a trial balance is a statement and can only be true on a particular date, so the heading states 'trial balance as at 31st March 1978'. We can use this first column to write in the ledger page or serial number, and this will be very useful for reference if we have to check back later for any reason. Since so many figures are involved in book-keeping, it is always wise to have as many references as possible so that figures can be traced back quickly and accurately.

Second column

The second column gives the name of the account, and includes 'cash at bank' and 'cash in hand' so that every transaction should be fully covered.

Last columns

The last columns give the familiar 'T' of debtor and creditor columns. The figure that is shown here is the balance on the particular account. If it is a credit balance (credit entries greater than debit entries) it is shown in the credit column. If it is a debit balance (debit entries greater than credit entries) it is shown in the debit column.

Balancing typical account

The balancing of each account consists of ruling off entries and finding out what the balance is. We will take the Capital A/c as a typical example:

Dr.   CAPITAL ACCOUNT – J.KABURU   Cr.

Date	Particulars	Amount	Date	Particulars	Amount
			1 March	Cash	1 000
			1 March	Pick up truck	1 200

Two entries

There are two entries in this account, both of which are on the credit side. This means that Mr J. Kaburu is owed

126

money by Kaburu Builders to cover the cash ($1,000) and the pick-up truck (value $1,200) which he has put into the firm to get it started.

Ruling off
The next step is to 'rule off' the account, which means drawing horizontal lines on the debtor and creditor sides of the account. These should be at the same level, and just below the lowest entry.

Total highest side
Then we total up both sides and write in the highest total *only*. In the case of this particular account there are no entries on the debit side, so the figure of $2,200 is written below the horizontal line on the credit side.

CAPITAL ACCOUNT - J.KABURU

Dr. | | | | | Cr.

Date	Particulars	Amount	Date	Particulars	Amount
			1 March	Cash	1000
			1 March	Pick up truck	1200
					2200

Transfer total
Since we are conducting a trial *balance*, we know that the totals must be equal. Thus the next step is to transfer the total of $2,200 by writing this figure in on the debit side.

Balancing figure
But we cannot leave the account like this, because we have written in a total of $2,200 on the debit side but the entries on that side (in this case there are none at all) do not add up to that figure. Thus we must bring in a balancing figure to make sure that it adds up properly.

To balance c/d
The balancing figure is written in like an ordinary entry. The date is the date of the trial balance (usually the last day

of the month). The particular column is written 'To Balance c/d'. The amount is the figure that is needed to make the total correct, in this case $2,200. 'C/d' indicates that this sum has been carried forward to the trial balance.

Dr.   CAPITAL ACCOUNT - J.KABURU   **Cr.**

Date	Particulars	Amount	Date	Particulars	Amount
			1 March	Cash	1000
31 March	To balance c/d	2200	1 March	Pick up truck	1200
		2200			2200

By balance b/d

A double line has been drawn under the two totals to show that a balance has been made. The next period is then started off with an entry 'By Balance b/d' *on the opposite side of the c/d item* to show that the sum has been brought forward from the balance sheet to bring the account back to its original state.

Same procedure

The same procedure is applied to all the other accounts, so that a series of balancing items are available to be written in on the trial balance.

Mythical transactions

The trial balance is a sort of holding account, and the balancing entries in the ledger accounts can be seen as half of a series of mythical transactions. These transactions, like the real ones we have recorded up to now, have to obey the laws of double-entry book-keeping.

Equal and opposite

This means that if the balancing figure in the ledger account was a *debit* item, it must be covered by an equal and opposite *credit* item in the trial balance. Thus the entry for the Capital A/c in Kaburu Builder's Trial Balance is $2,200 on the credit side.

128

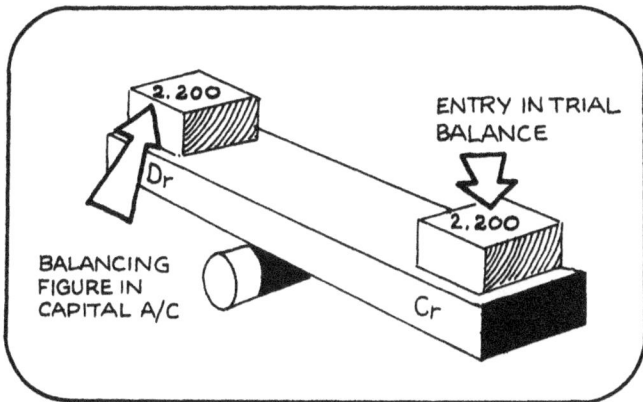

In the same way if the balancing figure in the ledger account is on the *credit* side, the entry in the trial balance is on the *debit* side.

Same total

Some accounts will show the same total on both the debit and credit sides. This can happen with a supplier's account which has been paid before the date of the trial balance or a customer's bill which has been settled. In a case like this the account is already in balance, so there is no need for a balancing figure or any entry to be made for that account in the trial balance.

Easy to make mistakes

In our example the trial balance worked out perfectly, with the totals on the debit and credit sides coming out as exactly equal. But this does not always happen. It is easy to make mistakes in book-keeping, either in making the original entries or taking out the trial balance. So we should give a little thought to what to do when the trial balance does not work out, showing that some form of human error has occurred.

Use a pencil

One sensible precaution is to use a pencil when first calculating the balancing figures on the ledger accounts, as this makes them easier to correct if a mistake does occur.

Where to start?

Let us suppose that we have made our trial balance, and we find to our dismay that the debit and credit totals are not the same. What is to be done? It will be necessary to check through the work. The first question is: 'Where to start?'.

Two sorts of errors

There are two sorts of errors that are likely to occur in making a trial balance:

1. Book-keeping mistakes
2. Extractor mistakes

Book-keeping mistakes

The most common book-keeping mistake is to post a credit item on the debit side or vice-versa. For example, if a supplier's account is credited with a sum of $70 when it should be debited, the debit side of the account (and therefore of the trial balance) will be short of double that amount: $140. One should be on the look-out for this sort of mistake if the difference between the debit and credit side is exactly divisible by *two.*

Another common mistake

Another common mistake is to transpose figures. For example $12 may be written as $21 or $45 may be written as $54. In this case, a sign that this type of mistake may have been made is when the difference between the debit and credit sides is divisible by *nine.*

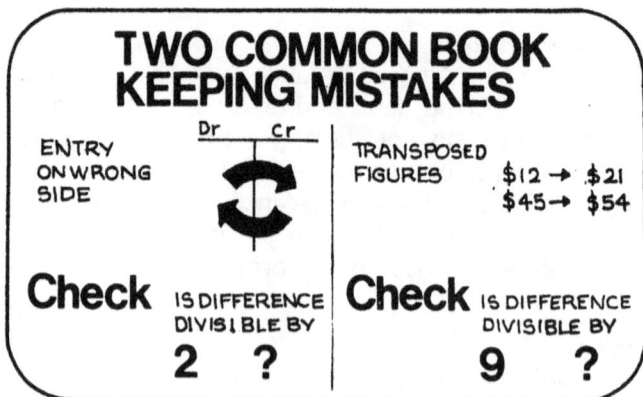

TWO COMMON BOOK KEEPING MISTAKES

ENTRY ON WRONG SIDE

Dr   Cr

TRANSPOSED FIGURES $12 → $21
$45 → $54

Check IS DIFFERENCE DIVISIBLE BY **2 ?**   **Check** IS DIFFERENCE DIVISIBLE BY **9 ?**

Another possibility

Yet another possibility is that a transaction has only been half-entered in the ledger accounts, and either the debit or credit half is missing.

Extraction mistakes

The other sort of mistakes can occur at the time of ruling off the accounts, calculating balancing figures and transferring balances to the trial balance. One mistake may be the simple omission of one of the relevant accounts, so the first thing to check is that all accounts have been balanced. It is also possible that a credit balance may have been placed on the debit side of the trial balance or vice-versa or that figures have been transposed ($12 for $21) at this stage.

Search with a system

Accountants learn by hard experience that it does not pay to look around the accounts wildly in the hope of coming across the mistake by chance. The best way is to search through systematically, eliminating one possibility after another like a detective investigating a crime. Everyone develops their own system, but one way to proceed is as follows:

First four steps

1. Find the difference between the debit and credit totals.
2. Ensure that all balances have been extracted and taken to the trial balance.
3. Re-check the trial balance totals.
4. Check that 'cash in hand' and 'cash at bank' have been included in the trial balance.

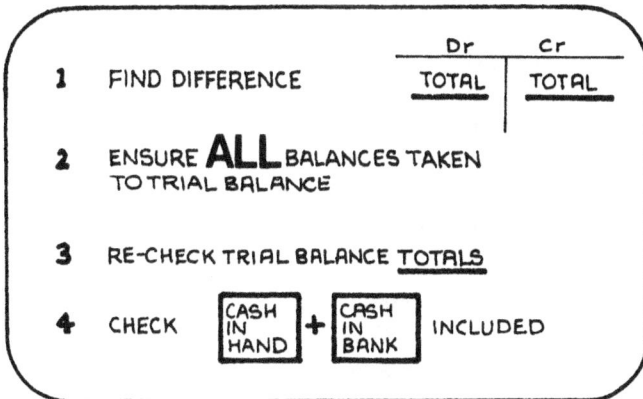

Next four steps

5. Check balance figure calculations and extraction of balances from ledger and transfer to trial balance. Make sure that balances have been correctly entered in debit or credit columns.

131

6. Divide the difference by two and see if any of the balances in the trial balance are equal to this figure. This might mean that a balance has been entered in the wrong column, giving an error of twice the balance.
7. Re-check the totals in the subsidiary books. Make sure that all items have been posted. Look carefully at any badly written figures.
8. If the difference is large, compare the trial balance figures with those for the corresponding period of the previous year. Many businesses have a fairly steady seasonal trading profit, and if one account is much higher or lower than usual it may be the one in error.

5   CHECK BALANCE FIGURE CACULATIONS

6   DIVIDE BY 2 : SEE IF ANY BALANCES EQUAL THIS FIGURE.

7   RE-CHECK TOTALS

8   COMPARE WITH FIGURES FOR PREVIOUS YEAR

Last four steps
9. Re-check postings of any amounts corresponding to the difference or half the difference.
10. Check figures that have been brought forward (b/fd) from previous account pages or the previous trial balance.
11. Start to check methodically through every posting of every item of every account. Start with nominal accounts.
12. If the error has still not been found, check postings to real accounts and finally personal accounts.

9   RE-CHECK POSTINGS EQUAL TO DIFFERENCE OR HALF DIFFERENCE

10   CHECK FIGURES   b /f d.

11   CHECK EVERY POSTING—START WITH NOMINAL A/Cs

12   CHECK REAL A/Cs –THEN PERSONAL A/Cs.

Trial balance agrees

At some stage on the journey through these twelve steps, a mistake (or perhaps even several mistakes) will have emerged and the debit and credit totals should now agree.

Not an absolute guarantee

This means that it is less likely that a mistake has been made, but we should remember that it is not an absolute guarantee that the book-keeping is correct.

Four more sorts of errors

This is because there are four more sorts of errors which do not affect the double entry book-keeping equation:

1. Compensating errors.
2. Clerical errors.
3. Errors of omission.
4. Errors of principle.

Compensating errors

If a mistake of $10 is made on one account and another mistake of $10 is made on a different account, they will cancel each other out as far as the trial balance is concerned. These errors may come to light if customers or suppliers complain or else should be found at the time of the audit.

Clerical errors

It is possible to simply post an entry to the wrong account, particularly where clients have rather similar names. For example, work done for Mr Nkosi may be charged to Mr Nkosa. No doubt Mr Nkosa will complain when he receives the bill for work which was not done for his benefit, although this is a very unsatisfactory way of finding the error.

Errors of omission

An error of omission occurs when an entry is completely forgotten and not entered in the subsidiary book. It is usually a charge for materials purchased on credit, and is likely to come to light when the supplier's statement is received and checked.

Errors of principle

An error of principle is the misrecording of a transaction. For example a liability may be treated as income or an item which should be posted to an expense account may be posted to an asset account. Errors of this kind may not be found out until the accounts are finally audited.

Errors can cost money

Needless to say, every effort should be made to carry out the book-keeping work properly in the first place. Not only do errors lead to a great deal of pointless work, but they can also cost money. Settlement of clients' accounts may be delayed or suppliers may withdraw credit facilities due to a failure to settle their accounts promptly.

How often to take a trial balance?

The final question is to decide how often to take a trial balance. We must certainly take a trial balance whenever final accounts have to be prepared. This will certainly be once a year, but may well be twice a year or even more often to give the managers a clearer idea of how the business is progressing.

Intermediate trial balances

However it may be worthwhile for the businessman to check his trial balance between final account periods. By taking these intermediate trial balances, he will trace errors more quickly and will avoid the prospect of a vast amount of work when a major balance has to be taken for the final accounts.

Analysis book method

Those contractors who rely on an analysis book for their accounting records will not need to worry about producing a trial balance as described above. They will naturally also lose the possibility of tracing detailed book-keeping errors that double entry book-keeping allows.

Checking with analysis book method

All that has to be done in the analysis book method is to total up the entries in each column. The check on the correctness of the entries and the addition comes from comparing the total in the bank column with the grand total of the totals in the subsidiary columns. This must be done for both the payments and receipts sides.

Annual statement

Using the analysis book method, analysis column totals are normally taken monthly. They can then be transferred to an annual statement with corresponding columns, and one horizontal line for each month of the year.

		BANK	SUBSIDIARY							
			1	2	3	4	5	6	7	8
		BANK	T_1	T_2	T_3	T_4	T_5	T_6	T_7	T_8

CHECK $\quad T_{BANK} = T_1 + T_2 + T_3 + T_4 + T_5 + T_6 + T_7 + T_8$

Chapter eight
Profit and Loss Accounts

Definition. Typical profit and loss account. Forecasting cash needs. Calculation of trading profit. Deciding on a dividend. Preparing the balance sheet. Danger of overtrading. Preparation of a funds flow statement.

Is the business profitable?

In putting a valuation on a business, whether it is involved with building contracting or anything else, we need to know two things. First we want to get some idea of the value of the assets which it owns and its liabilities. The balance sheet should help us with this. But we also need to know whether or not the business is making a profit.

Profit and loss A/c.

It is true that the balance sheet may give some indication. If there are large reserves on the profit and loss account, it is clear that profits must have been made at some time. But it does not tell us when they were made or how they were made. We therefore need a current profit and loss account to give a measure of the present financial efficiency of the firm.

Profit and loss A/c. periods

Unlike the balance sheet, which is a statement or 'snapshot' of the state of a business on a particular date, the profit and loss account covers a period. It is usual for the profit and loss account to cover a complete trading year, but it always runs from the date of one balance sheet to the next since balance sheets and profit and loss accounts depend on each other. Balance sheet dates can be chosen to suit the convenience of the company. But if the directors consider that a date has become inconvenient it is possible to run a profit and loss account for rather more or less than a year to bring the next balance sheet to a more convenient date.

Definition

A profit and loss account shows for a particular period of time either:

the surplus of income over costs which represent the amount by which the original capital has increased;

or: the loss, representing a reduction of the original capital.

Dividends or drawings

If a profit has been made, the profit and loss account will also show how much has been taken out of the business as dividends or drawings and how much has been left to boost working capital to allow additional business to be financed.

Typical profit and loss account

Later in this section we will see how the trading of the New Construction Company for a financial year is described in a balance sheet and profit and loss account. But first we can examine a typical profit and loss account to see what information it contains (see next page).

Once that is understood, we will know what we are aiming to produce when the final accounts have to be produced from ledger accounts or from the information contained in an analysis sheet.

Period

Since the profit and loss account covers a specific period, that period must be stated. Thus the heading shows that this particular account covers the period 1 January 1978 to 31 December 1978.

Sales and work done

The first item is described as 'sales and work done', and contains all relevant earnings during the financial year. It need not be separated further unless different kinds of activity are involved. The investment income is shown separately from sales and work done.

Expenses

Expenses should be separated out under suitable sub headings, and the profit and loss account shows the figures for this particular firm. The individual expenses are shown inset in a separate column, then added with the total placed under the main column. The difference between income and expenses gives the net trading profit for the financial (in this case also calender) year.

```
         TYPICAL PROFIT AND LOSS ACCOUNT

         Profit and Loss Account for the
         Year Ending 31st December 1978

                                                      £

Sales and Work Done                              52,500
Investment Income                                   640
                                 Total           53,140



Wages and Salaries               10,000
Materials                        20,800
Sub Contractors                   4,020
Plant & Vehicle Expenses          2,850
Bank Charges                        400
General Insurance                   850
Postages and Telephone              320
Printing and Stationery             180
Casual Labour                       520
Depreciation                      1,400          41,340

                          NET TRADING
                            PROFIT             11,800
```

Profit and loss appropriation account

The profit and loss account tells the reader how much profit (or loss) the company has made. We still need to know what happened to the profit. How much did the Government take in taxation? How much did the owners or shareholders decide to take out in dividends? What was left to put back into the business to finance increased business in the future? To find the answers to these questions we turn to the Profit and Loss Appropriation Account, which is a subsidiary account to the profit and loss account.

```
         TYPICAL  PROFIT  AND  LOSS  APPROPRIATION  ACCOUNT
                                                    $
Balance b/fd.                                    13,960
Add Net Trading Profit                           11,800
                                                 ──────
                                                 25,760
Deduct Taxation                                   4,860
                                                 ──────
                                                 20,900
Deduct Dividends                                  1,200
                                                 ──────
                         Balance c/d             19,700
                                                 ══════
```

Balance b/fd

The profit and loss appropriation account is an account like any other and must obey the normal book-keeping rules. Thus the first item is the balance brought forward from the previous balance sheet date. In this case the figure is $13,960 and represents profits earned and left unspent in the account up to 31st December 1977.

Add net trading profit

The Net Trading Profit calculated in the Profit and Loss Account must be added to the Balance b/fd to show the gross amount in the account before deductions.

Taxation

The first deduction is to cover taxation, which is calculated on the appropriate basis for the country concerned and preferably agreed with the taxation authority before the account is prepared.

Other deductions

This company has no loan capital or debentures outstanding but, if it had, the interest on them would have to be deducted before the directors could start to think about declaring a dividend.

Maximum possible dividend

Since there are no other deductions for payments to outsiders, the whole of the remaining $20,900 belongs to the shareholders. It is a fundamental principle of company law that dividends can only be paid out of profits. They cannot be paid out of capital. But they can be paid out of past profits as well as present profits. This means that the directors could go so far as to declare a maximum possible dividend of $20,900 if they so wish.

Keep within annual profit

But this would be a foolish policy. It would probably leave the company dangerously short of working capital. They would be wiser to work within the total net profit earned in the year which, after taxation, amounted to $6,940.

Small proportion in dividends

In fact they have chosen to distribute only a small proportion even of that in dividends. The dividend of $1,200 allows $5,740 to be reinvested in the business so that it will be strengthened and in a better position to earn even bigger profits in the years ahead.

New construction company

Now that we have seen what a profit and loss account looks like, we can return to the New Construction Company which we looked at in Chapter Six.

Partnership

The New Construction Company has started as a partnership. The first partner has a considerable practical experience of the building industry and is prepared to invest his savings of $2,000 in the new enterprise. The other partner is a more wealthy trader who is experienced in business and commerce, but who has little knowledge of the building industry. He is prepared to make $8,000 available to the new firm.

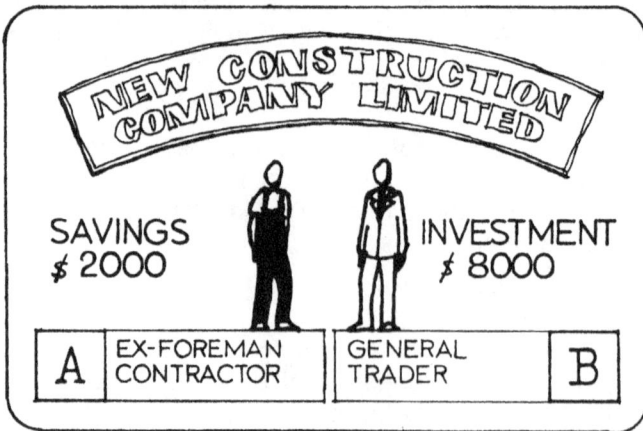

Total $10,000

Thus a total investment of $10,000 is available to the partners to finance their new enterprise.

A good partnership

We commented previously that, at first sight, this appears to be a partnership that stands a reasonably good chance of being successful. One man brings technical experience and a little capital. The other brings money as well as financial and commercial expertise.

Allocation of profits

Let us suppose that they decide that it would be best to trade as a limited company, thereby limiting their risk of losing money to the money that they put up and any guarantees that might be made to clients or suppliers. The first problem that they must face is to decide how to allocate profits and how to arrange the share capital.

Easiest approach

The easiest approach would be to form a company with $10,000 capital and allot 2,000 shares of $1 to Mr A and 8,000 of $1 to Mr B.

Unfair to A

But this would hardly be fair. It would mean that Mr A would be giving up a good job and investing all his life savings but would at best only get a fifth of the annual profit.

Not best for B

Even Mr B would not really gain by this arrangement. It would mean that Mr A, upon whom he would rely to run the business from day to day, would not have sufficient incentive to devote all his time to the business. In fact he might become jealous of Mr B getting the lion's share of declared profits and be tempted to take money from the business dishonestly or accept bribes from merchants or sub contractors.

Share profits equally

The two men have discussed the problem. They agree that they both have special skills to contribute as well as the money that they will put into the business, and that it would be only fair that they should have equal financial incentives. Thus they have to find some way of organising the business that will allow them to share the profits equally.

Equity

It is only the ordinary shares in a company that constitute the 'equity' which entitles holders to a share in the profits after all expenses have been met. Holders of debentures, loan stock and preference shares are all entitled to be paid before any dividend on the ordinary shares is considered, but they are normally not given any further chance to share in profits.

Equity shared equally

Mr A and Mr B therefore agree that the equity should be shared equally, and each man should take up 2,000 ordinary shares of $1. This produces a total of $4,000 for the New Construction Company Ltd. In order to provide the full $10,000 that will be needed to get the business started, Mr B says he is prepared to lend the extra $6,000 to the company until it is properly established.

A loan

Mr B is planning to retire in ten years time. He intends to retire and live in his home town, so a ten year period is agreed for the $6,000 loan. This should give the firm sufficient time to get itself established on a profitable basis, and make sufficient retentions from profits to repay the loan without affecting the basic strength of the business. In order to give the firm a better chance of success, Mr B says that he is prepared to accept a rather low interest rate of 5 per cent on his money, which is much more favourable to the company than the commercial rate of interest charged by a bank.

NCC Ltd.

HOW TO SHARE THE PROFITS?
HOW TO ARRANGE SHARE CAPITAL?

EASIEST APPROACH:
A. ($2000)   2000 SHARES
B ($8000)   8000 SHARES

BETTER WAY:
A. 2000 ORDINARY SHARES AT $1
B 2000 ORDINARY SHARES AT $1
+$6000 of 5% LOAN STOCK to be repaid in 1988

Thus the initial capital of the company consists of:

Equal share capital
 Mr A 2,000 Ord. shares of $1
 Mr B 2,000 Ord. shares of $1
  and $6,000 of 5% loan stock to be repaid in 1988.

Forming the company
 We will assume that the cost of legal fees, etc. for forming the company is $100, so $9,900 can be deposited in the company's bank account.

	$
ISSUED CAPITAL	
A. 2000 ORDINARY SHARES of $1	
B. 2000 ORDINARY SHARES of $1	4000
LOANS	
5% LOAN CAPITAL to be repaid in 1987	6000
TOTAL	10000
COST OF FORMING COMPANY	100
CASH AT BANK	9900
TOTAL	10000

Even split between fixed and current assets
 In Chapter Six it was reported that the directors had decided to split their funds evenly between fixed and current assets.

Fixed assets
 They decided that fixed assets should be purchased or allocated as follows:

FIXED ASSETS

LAND AND BUILDINGS	$2000
OFFICE EQUIPMENT	200
PLANT AND TOOLS	800
MOTOR VEHICLES	1200
PLANT RESERVES	800
	$5000

Current assets

Since $100 of the original $10,000 has been spent on forming the company, this leaves $4,900 for current assets. This sum of $4,900 will circulate in the business as working capital, funding wages, materials, plant hire and incidental expenses on contracts, until these are financed by payments received from clients.

```
CURRENT ASSETS

FOR: WAGES
     MATERIALS          UNTIL PAYMENT
     PLANT HIRE         RECEIVED
     INCIDENTAL         FROM CLIENT
       EXPENSES
                   ORIGINAL CASH      9900
                   FIXED ASSETS       5000
     LEAVES FOR  CURRENT ASSETS      4900
```

$4,900 maximum

The directors will have to bear this figure of $4,900 in mind as they tender for work and ensure that the jobs which they take on will not require finance in excess of this sum at any time.

Forecasting cash needs

The cash requirement for each job can be assessed with the aid of the programme for carrying out the work. The best way to do this is to plot the cumulative payments on a job against the time scale of the job. The method is shown in outline in the illustration below:

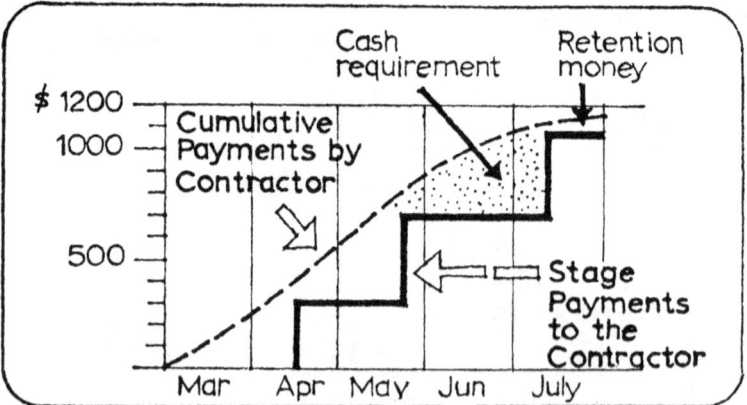

Cash flow

This one diagram, providing it has been drawn up accurately and realistically, shows the cash flow on this contract from day to day right through from commencement to completion. For example, the difference between total payments made up to May 1st and the money received from clients up to that day gives the value of cash tied up in the contract on that day.

Each job separately then total

All major contracts should be dealt with in this way, but the cash flow on smaller jobs can usually be estimated reasonably accurately on the basis of experience. Once this has been done, the total cash requirement of the company on any particular day can be determined. This in turn can be drawn in the form of a diagram, to show an overall cash flow forecast for the company which is of great value in budgeting. An illustration of what the cash flow forecast for the New Construction Company Ltd may look like is shown below:

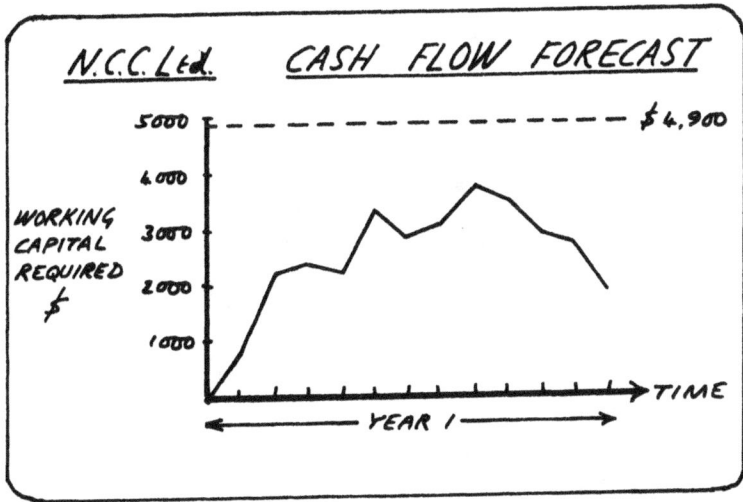

N.C.C. Ltd. CASH FLOW FORECAST

Within $4,900 available

It is clear that, providing the forecast is accurate, the sum of $4,900 which is available in the bank account will be sufficient. Thus it seems likely that the business will be in a position to trade successfully in its first year of operation.

Forward a year

Now that we know how the company has started, let us jump forward a year and see what has been achieved during

145

the first full year of trading. Then we can produce the set of final accounts so that the financial situation can be properly analysed.

Five jobs finished

During the year the company has completed five jobs worth a total of $6,000 at a direct cost of $5,200. However two clients have not yet made their payments in full and $1,200 is outstanding on these two jobs. Thus actual receipts on Jobs 1-5 are as yet only $4,800.

Sixth contract

The company is at the moment in the middle of its sixth contract, which is rather larger than anything they have tackled before. Payments to date on this job are $200. Work in progress (including materials on site) for which the client has yet to make payment has been valued at $2,800. So far wage, materials and other payments of $1,500 have been made and creditors will have to be paid a further $450 when their accounts fall due for payment.

NCC Ltd.

FIRST YEAR'S TRADING

JOBS Nos. 1-5 (FINISHED)

VALUE	$ 6000
COST	5200
RECEIVED	4800

JOB No. 6 (IN PROGRESS)

PAYMENTS RECEIVED	$ 200
WORK IN PROGRESS	2800
WAGES ETC. PAID	1500
CREDITORS	450

Setting it out clearly

One of the jobs of the accountant is to set out figures such as these in a clear and concise way to that the financial position of the company can be clearly understood.

Payments in and out

The first step is to work out the total of payments made and received, drawing on the information contained in the ledger. For the New Construction Company Ltd these will be:

Contract Payments Made		Contract Payments Received	
Jobs 1-5	$5,200	Job 1-5	$4,800
Job 6	1,500	Job 6	200
	$6,700		$5,000

CONTRACT PAYMENTS MADE

JOBS Nos. 1-5		5200
JOB No. 6		1500
	TOTAL	6700

CONTRACT PAYMENTS RECEIVED

JOBS Nos. 1-5		4800
JOB No. 6		200
	TOTAL	5000

Other payments

Then it is necessary to list any other payments made or received. For example the money deposited at the bank may have attracted interest, and premiums on insurance policies have to be paid.

Example payments

For the purposes of this example we will neglect these small items (although of course in real life they cannot be neglected). We assume that there are no additional receipts, but that the following payments have been made:

1. Fee to Mr A who has been working, full-time
   for the business — $1,000
2. Loan interest to Mr B —
   5 per cent of $6,000 — $300

147

Check cash at bank

We can now check whether our calculations so far have been made correctly by working out the value of cash at the bank:

Total Payments		Total Receipts	
Contracts	6,700	Contracts	5,000
Director's fees	1,000		
Loan interest	300		
	8,000		5,000

TOTAL PAYMENTS

CONTRACTS		6700
DIRECTORS FEE		1000
LOAN INTEREST		300
	TOTAL	8000

TOTAL RECEIPTS

CONTRACTS		5000
	TOTAL	5000

INITIAL BANK BALANCE	4900
NET PAYMENTS TOTAL	3000
PRESENT BALANCE	1900

Bank balance

The initial bank balance was $4,900. Net payments are $8,000 minus $5,000 or $3,000. Thus the present bank balance should be $1,900 according to our calculations. This figure should be checked against the bank statement to ensure that the calculations are accurate.

Calculation of trading profit

The next stage of the calculations is to determine the amounts owed *to* the company and *by* the company. In practice the ledger (if properly kept) will reveal these figures. They will be found by adding up the amounts owed by and owing to the company for each individual account.

In the present example, the figures for the New Construction Company Ltd are as follows:

Owed by the Company		Owed to the Company	
Creditors	450	Debtors	1,200
		Work in progress	2,800
	450		4,000

OWED BY THE COMPANY		OWED TO THE COMPANY	
CREDITORS	450	DEBTORS	1200
		WORK IN PROGRESS	2800
	450		4000
CONTRACT PAYMENTS	6700	CONTRACT RECEIPTS	5000
TOTAL	7150	TOTAL	9000

Contract payments and receipts

The first task is to determine the gross trading profit, which means that director's fees and loan interest can be left for the time being. To calculate gross trading profit we add in contract payments and receipts as follows:

Owed by the company	450	Owed to the company	4,000
Contract payments	6,700	Contract receipts	5,000
	7,150		9,000

Gross trading profit

Thus assuming no change in fixed assets and ignoring depreciation for a moment, the gross trading profit is $1,850 which looks reasonably satisfactory.

Depreciation

The problem of depreciation was dealt with in detail in a previous section. It will be remembered that accounting

149

assumes that some portion of an asset is used up during each year of its life. Thus the various ways of calculating depreciation start with a decision on the choice of method by which one can estimate what portion of the initial value of an asset should be treated as an expense in any given year.

Changing asset into annual expense

Thus depreciation is actually a way of changing an asset into a series of annual expenses. The intention being that at the end of the asset's life the total of the annual expenses should be equal to the original cost of the asset. If the asset is in fact sold at some stage there will be a balancing charge, either credit or debit, depending on whether the price realised is more or less than the depreciated figure.

Straight line depreciation

The simplest method of calculating depreciation is the 'straight line method'. This means that it is assumed that the asset loses its initial value at a constant rate over the whole of its life.

Easy to calculate

Depreciation is very easy to calculate by this method. The first step is to establish the life of each individual asset or group of assets in years. Then the cost of the asset is divided by the life in years to give the annual depreciation, which is charged as an expense in the profit and loss account for each year of the life of the asset.

New Construction Company

The figures for the New Construction Company Ltd are as shown below, the total depreciation in the first year being $360:

DEPRECIATION			
ASSET	Initial Value	Life in Years	Writeoff Each Yr
	(1)	(2)	(3)
Land & Buildings	2000	50	40
Office Equipment	200	10	20
Plant & Equipment	800	8	100
Motor Vehicles	1200	6	200
Plant Reserves (not used)	800	--	--
			360

Deduct depreciation

The gross trading profit was calculated to be $1,850. Depreciation of $360 must be deducted from that, leaving a balance of $1,490.

Pay interest

Then $300 loan interest has to be paid to Mr B ($6,000 at 5 per cent) leaving $1,190.

Director's fees

Out of this Mr A, who has worked full time for the company, is to receive a fee of $1,000 which leaves only $190.

Taxation

We will assume that taxation takes $40 of the residue, so the Company has in fact ended the year just $150 better off than when it started.

PROFIT & LOSS FOR YEAR 1

OVERALL PROFIT OF N.C.C.	1850
DEDUCT DEPRECIATION OF FIXED ASSETS	360
	1490
DEDUCT INTEREST ON $6000 5% LOAN	300
	1190
DEDUCT FEE TO WORKING DIRECTOR	1000
NET PROFIT BEFORE TAXATION	190
TAX	40
BALANCE TRANSFERRED TO P&L ACCOUNT	150

Profit and loss account

This sum of $150 can now be transferred to the Profit and Loss Account, from which the balance will be transferred to the Balance Sheet. Profit and loss accounts are kept separate from other accounts for several reasons, but most importantly because dividends can be paid to shareholders only if there is sufficient cash in the profit and loss account.

Dividends out of profit and loss account

Thus a company with an adverse balance on profit and loss account has to clear that loss before it can pay a dividend.

Equally, a company with accumulated profits from previous years is permitted to pay a dividend from these funds, even if it makes a loss in the year in question.

Started with adverse balance

The New Construction Company Ltd started the year with an adverse balance on its profit and loss account, representing the $100 that had to be spent in legal fees, etc. for the formation of the company.

$50 left

This figure must be deducted from the profit earned in the first year of operation, so the actual balance at the end of the year is $150 less $100, which is $50.

Calculating possible dividend

This sum could be paid as a dividend, if the directors so decided. The equity capital of the company is $4,000 so a dividend of:

$$\frac{(50)}{(4000)} \times 100 = 1\frac{1}{4} \text{ per cent}$$

could be paid.

CALCULATING THE DIVIDEND

EQUITY CAPITAL OF THE COMPANY $ 4000
BALANCE ON P. & L. ACCOUNT $ 50

$$\frac{50}{4000} \times 100 = 1\frac{1}{4}\%$$

THEREFORE: A DIVIDEND OF $1\frac{1}{4}\%$
COULD BE PAID

Growth needs

But if all profits are taken in dividends each year the company will never be able to grow. Even more important, where a company has a high proportion of loan capital, the directors should remember that the time will come for it to be repaid.

A buffer

Also it is wise to build up the profit and loss account so as to provide a cushion in case the company has to face hard times in the future.

No dividend

Thus the directors decide not to pay a dividend for the first year, so the Company will enter its second year in a slightly stronger position.

First NCC Ltd profit and loss account

Thus no alteration needs to be made to the profit and loss appropriation account to allow for dividend payments, and the first profit and loss account for the New Construction Company Ltd may be as shown on the following page.

Sub-heads

Although information on individual expenses has not been made available, some possible sub-heads for expenses have been shown in order to produce a more realistic document.

Fees and depreciation

The reader will note that the figures for Directors' Fees and Depreciation have been included in the expenses sub-heads of the Profit and Loss Account. This is done because they are direct operating expenses and must therefore be deducted before any decision as to the allocation of Net Trading Profit can be made.

Last check on cash position

It is wise to make a final check on the cash position at this stage:

Initial cash at Bank		4,900
Net profit on trading		150
		———
		5,050
Owed by the Company:		
1. Creditors	450	
2. Taxation	40	
3. Depreciation transfer to plant reserve	360	850
	———	———
		5,900
Owed to the Company:		
1. Debtors	1200	
2. Work in progress	2800	4,000
	———	———
		1,900

NEW CONSTRUCTION COMPANY LTD

Profit and Loss Account for the Year Ending
31st December 1978

			£
Sales and Work Done			9000
Wages and Salaries	)		
Materials	)		
Sub Contractors	)		
Plant & Vehicle Expenses	)		
Bank Charges	)	7,150	
General Insurance	)		
Postages and Telephone	)		
Printing and Stationery	)		
Casual Labour	)		
Director's Fees		1,000	
Depreciation		360	8510
	NET TRADING PROFIT		490

Profit and Loss Appropriation Account

Adverse Balance b/fd		(100)
Add Net Trading Profit		490
		390
Deduct Loan Interest		300
		90
Deduct Taxation		40
	Balance c/d	50

Correct balance

This agrees with the previous calculation and the actual bank balance, so the recent calculations seem to be correct.

Constant checking

Constant checking of calculations may seem boring and unnecessary at first, but it is really very worthwhile to check calculations frequently as mistakes can be identified and corrected more easily.

CHECKING CASH POSITION

INITIAL CASH AT BANK		4900
NET PROFIT ON TRADING		150
		5050
OWED BY THE COMPANY:		
1.CREDITORS	450	
2.TAXATION	40	
3.TRANSFER to PLANT RES	360	850
		5900
OWED TO THE COMPANY:		
1. DEBTORS	1200	
2. WORK IN PROGRESS	2800	4000
		1900

Balance sheet

We now have all the information necessary to construct a balance sheet. The previous year's figures are shown against those for the current year for easy comparison. The vertical form of presentation has been chosen on this occasion (see next page).

Net current assets

Using the vertical form of presentation, the current assets (Work in Progress, Debtors and Cash at Bank) are listed first and a sub-total obtained. Then current liabilities (Creditors, Depreciation and Tax) are listed and their sub-total is deducted to give Net Current Assets.

Fixed assets and liabilities

The next stage of the calculation is to deal with fixed assets and liabilities. For ease of explanation, plant reserves have been shown among the fixed assets, although they would normally appear as part of the Cash at Bank in current assets.

155

Owner's investment

Assets less liabilities measure the owner's investment, and the breakdown of that is shown below the horizontal line.

NEW CONSTRUCTION COMPANY LTD				
BALANCE SHEET AS AT 31ST DECEMBER 1978				
	THIS YEAR		LAST YEAR	
	$	$	$	$
Work in progress	2,800		–	
Debtors	1,200			
Cash at Bank	1,900	5,900	4,900	4,900
LESS Current Liabilities				
Creditors	450			
Depreciation set aside for plant reserves	360			
Tax	40	850		
NET CURRENT ASSETS		5,050		4,900
FIXED ASSETS				
Land & buildings	1,960		2,000	
Office equipment	180		200	
Plant and tools	700		800	
Motor Vehicles	1,000		1,200	
Plant reserves (incl. depreciation)	1,160	5,000	800	5,000
		10,050		9,900
LESS Loan Capital		6,000		6,000
		4,050		3,900
Represented by:-				
Issued Capital 4000 Ord. Shares of $1		4,000		4,000
Balance (deficit) on P & L Account		50		(100)
		4,050		3,900

Real balance

Thus N.C.C. Ltd. has a real cash balance in its bank account of $1,900 together with a plant reserve of $1,160 so there is a total of $3,060 available for investment in current and/or fixed assets.

156

More capacity

This is quite a comfortable position for a company of this size and will permit the company to take on a little more work in the coming year. It also means that the company will survive if it faces a crisis such as a bad debt by a client or dishonesty by employees.

Overtrading

One of the most prominent reasons for bankruptcies among construction and building companies is overtrading. This applies in almost all countries. Contracts are hard to come by and it is difficult to refuse work. Builders tend to be optimistic by nature. There are so many uncertainties that they have to be! But there is a difference between optimism and blind foolishness.

Be ready for setbacks

Thus the optimist should be realistic enough to realise that, no matter how carefully thought out his plan, on almost every contract something will go wrong. If he is a good manager, he will correct errors quickly, but unless there is enough money in the bank a series of small problems can cripple a company. Thus we hope that the Directors of the N.C.C. will preserve a reasonable cash position.

Funds flow statement

One way of keeping track of the trends in a firm's finances is to produce a 'funds flow statement'. This shows clearly how the use of money in a business has changed from one year to the next. Since N.C.C. Ltd. has only been in operation for a year it is not very useful in this case, but its funds flow statement is illustrated on the next page as an example.

Using a funds flow statement

In general a funds flow statement can be very helpful to management in highlighting any major increase in debtors or work in progress. If debtors have increased more than turnover, it may be that clients should be pressed to pay more quickly or that certain clients are poor commercial risks. If work in progress has increased disproportionately, it may be worthwhile checking whether interim and final certificates are being prepared and submitted promptly enough.

Money costs money

The contractor must always remember that money is just another of the resources which he has to have in order to build, and that as a good manager he must use it effectively so as to minimise costs. Money costs money, since interest rates are high on borrowings and surplus cash could usually be put to more profitable use in expanding the business.

NEW CONSTRUCTION COMPANY LTD

FUNDS FLOW STATEMENT
AS AT 31st DECEMBER 1978

Source of Funds

Profit	150	
Depreciation	360	510
Increase in Creditors & Accrued Expenses		850
		1,360

Application of Funds

Increase in Debtors	1,200	
Increase in Work in Progress	2,800	4,000
Decrease in Cash Funds		(2,640)
Cash at start		5,700
Cash at end		3,060

Chapter Nine
Reading and Comparison of Accounts

A standard for comparison. Assessing value. Comparing current with previous period. Comparing current period with budget. Comparison between contracts. Limitations. Ratio analysis. Calculating return on capital. Calculating marginal profit on marginal capital employed.

Interpreting accounts

We have now built up a balance sheet and profit and loss account from scratch. But we have already agreed that there is more to accounting than just 'keeping records'.

A snapshot

The balance sheet provides a 'snapshot' of your business on a particular day. If it has been prepared carefully and honestly, it will give a clear and accurate picture of the strengths and weaknesses of the firm. But just as an architect's drawing has little meaning for the layman (who will be unable to build a picture in his mind from the plans, elevations and details) so the balance sheet and profit and loss account appear as a dry and meaningless mass of numbers to the uninitiated.

The picture tells a story

There is an old saying that 'every picture tells a story'. To the businessman who understands the 'language' of accountancy, every balance sheet tells a story. In fact it is reported that Lord Thomson, who built up one of the largest groups of newspapers in the world, preferred a set of balance sheets to a novel at his bedside!

Figures alone are not enough

Of course there are some figures that are easy to see in the profit and loss account and balance sheet of any organisation. But by themselves they don't tell us very much. For example, we may see that a firm made a profit of $10,000 in its last financial year. For a new one-man business that would be a very good result. But for a large international contractor it would be a disaster! Thus we have to search for some simple techniques to help us judge whether figures are good or bad.

A standard for comparison

Whenever we wish to judge anything, whether it be length, weight, temperature or any other quality, we must first provide a standard of comparison. We may say that a motor car is expensive, but we can only judge its cost in relation to the price of other cars in the same showroom, or other prices in the catalogue or the price we paid two years ago.

Assessing value

We have the same problem in assessing the value of a building firm. The balance sheet is a very important document, but in isolation it is meaningless. We have to set some standard by which the figures can be judged. It is by comparing one set of figures with another, as we compare the length of an object with a set of standard lengths on a ruler, that we can measure the value of the figures that we have to assess.

Possible comparisons

Suppose we have some figures relating to output and profit of some particular firm for some particular period. Let us consider some possible comparisons that we might usefully make.

Compare current with previous period

A start might be made by comparing the work done last week with the work done this week, or the work done this month with the work done last month. These comparisons can usefully be made for each separate contract to see how individual site managers are performing, and a similar comparison can be done to gauge the performance of the firm as a whole.

Extraneous factors

Allowance must of course be made for extraneous factors, such as weather conditions, holidays or delays in material deliveries which might adversely affect production in either the current or the previous period.

Current period with last year

A good way of minimising the distortion of figures by seasonal factors is to make a comparison with a corresponding set of figures for the same period in the previous year. For example we might compare the output per man this week with the output per man in the similar week of the previous year.

Current period with budget

Whenever possible a businessman should prepare financial and output budgets so that he knows where he is going and can work to a plan. The budget can be a powerful tool in the hands of an experienced businessman, and a comparison of output and profits for the current period against budgeted figures can be extremely helpful. Budgets are made to be *used,* not filed away. The more frequently a businessman compares figures with his budget, the sooner he will be able to find discrepancies.

Budget is there to be used!

Very often it is easy to stop a dangerous trend (loss of productivity, increasing bank overdraft, etc.) in its early stages, but if it goes on unchecked the business could be seriously harmed. It is no use supplying a doctor or a nurse with a thermometer, if they cannot be bothered to take their patient's temperature. The budget is the businessman's thermometer, it is there to be *used*!

Comparison between contracts

Where a number of comparable contracts are undertaken by a single organisation, either in the private or the public sector, there are always useful lessons to be drawn from differences in performance between them. It is very much better to be objective than subjective in judging how individual site managers and foremen perform, and in fact most people perform better if they know that their qualities (and deficiencies) are being noticed. A proper system of performance appraisal also assists the proprietor as the business expands, as it gives guidance as to which of his employees most deserves promotion.

Comparison between firms

A further possible comparison can be with typical figures for other firms in the building industry. This is particularly relevant when firms are thinking of merging or amalgamating so that they will be able to tackle larger contracts. Bargaining for terms between proprietors or shareholders will be based on their analysis of the financial strengths and weaknesses of the business involved.

Previous annual accounts

A comparison of the most recent set of annual accounts with previous editions can also prove interesting. Trends in profit, turnover, absolute and relative costs can yield useful clues as to whether the company is steadily improving its trading position or is in a state of decline. This comparison can be made more effective by the use of ratio analysis techniques which will be discussed later in this chapter.

Limitations

Although we can learn a good deal about the health of a business by taking a careful look at its balance sheets and profit and loss accounts for a period of years, we must also remember that they cannot tell the whole story. The limitations are inherent in the assumptions that we make in preparing the accounts in the first place, without which a comparable and systematic system of keeping financial records would not be possible.

Only in monetary terms

The first and most obvious limitation results from the fact that accounts only report on events which can be expressed in or translated into direct monetary terms. Thus assets such as trucks, mixers and dumpers will appear as assets in the balance sheet. But other vital assets such as a shrewd and knowledgeable manager or a well-trained and loyal work force cannot be directly valued and shown. Equally, of course, a thoroughly incompetent and useless manager cannot be shown amongst the liabilities!

No account of inflation

Most commonly used accounting techniques take no account of the effects caused by inflation, although methods of making adjustments for inflationary effects are now being discussed and sometimes inflation-adjusted accounts are added as an appendix to the annual accounts for purposes of comparison. But in general the basis of recording assets is to take their cost price and make a (hopefully) appropriate adjustment for depreciation year by year.

Depreciation

Depreciation is a way of writing off a proportion of the cost price in each year, so that zero value will be shown in the accounts when the time comes for the asset to be discarded as worn out and useless. Thus the depreciated 'value' of any particular asset in a balance sheet does not necessarily give a true indication of its market value.

Value as a going concern

Indeed market value is not even a certainty. If I own a second hand concrete mixer with a depreciated 'value' of $400 my attitude to selling it will be based on whether I am still in the building business. If I had a contract which involves a great deal of concrete work I would not be likely to agree to sell it even if I was offered $600. But if I have decided to give up building, I might be pleased to accept an offer of only $250 to get it off my hands. Thus to give a consistent basis, assets are always valued on the assumption that the business is a going concern.

Cannot foretell the future

A further point to remember is that annual accounts deal only with what has happened in the past. That may or may not be a reasonable indication of what is likely to happen in the future. For example a company may have made a profit of $10,000 in 1976, but that is no guarantee that it will do as well in 1977. However these past records do provide a reasonable starting point for the financial analyst, providing he also examines any changing circumstances that may affect future results.

Alternative methods

Then the reader of a balance sheet must also remember that different accountants can quite legitimately use different methods to calculate assets, liabilities and profits. For example, various methods of calculating depreciation can be used depending on personal judgement of which method is most realistic. Stock can be valued on the LIFO (last in, first out) method or the FIFO (first in, first out) method. Under the former method, stocks will reflect original costs for items that are always kept in stock. Under the latter method, the stocks will reflect more recent costs and so individual items will be more highly valued.

Extremely useful

Despite these limitations, accounting information remains an extremely useful way of quickly finding out about the performance of a business.

Objectives

Before we start to make measurements we must have a reasonably clear idea of the financial objectives of a business. Most businesses have two basic financial objectives:

1. To earn an acceptable return on money invested in the business;
2. While doing so, to maintain a sound financial position and minimise risk.

Figures alone not enough

This means that the figures in the profit and loss account, by themselves, may not tell the whole story. If a firm had recently bought expensive additional plant and machinery, the directors would rightly be very disappointed if no additional work was obtained and carried out, and the company failed to earn additional profits. Thus, if a firm can earn $1,000 profit when it has $5,000 assets, we might reasonably expect it to earn $2,000 on $10,000 assets.

Ratios required

Thus a company may increase its profits by 50 per cent, but be performing less well than one with a 10 per cent increase. The figures alone are not enough. It is only when we use ratios, that clear trends begin to appear.

Example: Year one

Suppose a building company completes work worth $10,000 in year 1, with expenses as follows:

	$
Materials	4,000
Plant	2,000
Labour	1,500
Overheads	1,500
	$9,000

Example: Year two

In year 2, it carries out $15,000 of work:

	$
Materials	6,000
Plant	3,000
Labour	2,250
Overheads	2,250
	$13,500

Constant percentage relationship

When we compare the two sets of figures we see that all expenses show a constant relationship with total work done:

	%
Materials	40
Plant	20
Labour	15
Overheads	15
	90%

Example: Year three

Now, suppose $20,000 of work is carried out in year 3 with expenses as follows:

	$
Materials	8,000
Plant	4,000
Labour	3,500
Overheads	3,000
	$18,500

New ratios

We analyse the ratios as follows:

	%
Materials	40
Plant	20
Labour	17.5
Overheads	15
	92.5%

Gross profit unchanged

Materials, plant and overheads all remain in the same proportion to overheads, but a more than proportionate increase in labour costs has taken place. We now know why, despite an increase of $5,000 in work done, gross profit is unchanged at $1,500.

Higher labour costs

The whole of the profit on this increased turnover has been eaten up by labour costs. This must be investigated by the directors. It may be caused by higher wages, lower productivity or perhaps low tendering to expand turnover regardless of cost.

May be a good reason

There may be a quite acceptable reason for an increase in any cost percentage. Higher plant costs may lead to valuable savings in labour cost. Contracts may be taken in a different field of activity, such as road construction, where plant and labour costs are often higher than in building. All we know is that where the percentage changes, the reason should be investigated.

We can now examine some ratios for our typical business:

Gross profit ratio

The net trading profit for the year was $490. It would be useful for the owners to know the percentage profit on each $100 of work that they carry out, so that they will have a yardstick against which to estimate for and judge future work.

The work carried out in the year was as follows:

Jobs 1-5	$6,000
Job 6	$3,000
	$9,000

Turnover

This total of $9,000 is known as the *annual turnover.*
Therefore profit ratio =

$$\frac{490}{9000} \times 100 = 5\frac{1}{2} \text{ per cent}$$

That is, out of every $100 of work done the firm made $5½ profit.

Gross profit

It is most important that we remember that this ratio is based on trading profit, and it must be large enough to cover loan interest and taxation before any net profit is left for dividends or to plough back into the business.

166

Compare sections

Where a company is involved in a number of different areas of business — for example building, civil engineering and minor works, it is interesting to compare profit rates on turnover in each of these sections of the firm's activity.

Small jobs — high profit margin

You will usually find that small jobs carry the highest profit margin, and as the size of job increases the profit percentage drops. This is one of the difficulties faced by an expanding business.

There is a temptation for the directors of such a business to say "We are a big business now and we will concentrate on contracts over $10,000 and ignore small jobbing work — it is too much trouble". What they might not realise is that it was the high profit margins on jobbing work that were providing practically all their profit.

Net profit ratio

This is probably the most important ratio as far as the owners of a business are concerned.

Profitability

The long term success or failure of a business depends on the amount of profit it earns. A family may put money into their business for sentimental reasons, but the Bank Manager will not be so amenable. The ability of a business to raise additional capital will largely depend on its record of profitability.

Return on capital

The net profit is usually regarded as the return on capital of the firm. For comparison purposes, it is useful to express this as a percentage of the capital invested in the business. However, we must be wary of the term 'capital', for it is capable of a number of interpretations, and when comparing ratios we must ensure that the definitions are the same.

(A) Net Profit/Capital Invested

The definition of capital here is the equity capital shown in the Balance Sheet as Issued Capital. In the case of N.C.C. Ltd. this is $4,000. Thus our profit ratio is:

$$\frac{(150)}{(4,000)} \times 100 = 3.75 \text{ per cent}$$

Current return on original capital

This represents the current return on the original capital, and serves as a guide to the maximum amount of dividend that could be distributed to shareholders. (You will of course remember that the directors of the N.C.C. Ltd. decided not to pay a dividend due to the adverse balance on profit and loss account.)

The main value of this ratio is that it shows the wisdom or otherwise of the original investment. We should note, however, that its value declines with the years because it only shows the *current* profit in relation to the *original* investment, but retained profits and an increase in the value of buildings and land may mean that the present value of the investment is very different. Thus, we have another ratio to indicate *current* efficiency.

Current efficiency

We know that businesses seldom distribute the whole of their profits as dividends. In order to allow their companies to grow and take on more contracts, they retain a proportion and place it either to reserve or keep it in the profit and loss account.

Current capital

Either way, this proportion of the profits over the years still belongs to the ordinary shareholders. It simply means that instead of spending this excess money or investing it in another business, they have allowed it to be invested in the original business. It is therefore *their* capital, even if they have no additional share certificates to prove it.

Another example

Let us consider a company with:

Issued Capital — 10,000 Ord. Shs of $1	10,000
Reserves	10,000
Balance on Profit and Loss Account	5,000
	25,000

Exercise

If the net profit is $4,000 let us calculate:

1. Ratio Net Profit/Capital Invested?
2. Ratio Net Profit/Capital Employed?

Answers

1. $\dfrac{(4,000)}{(10,000)} \times 100 = 40$ per cent

2. $\dfrac{(4,000)}{(25,000)} \times 100 = 16$ per cent

In the case of the N.C.C. Ltd. the two ratios would be much the same because the company has only just started to trade but, if it is successful in the future, they will soon become as different as in the example above.

Profit is essential

Before we go on to consider the future of the N.C.C. Ltd., it is worth stating that there is nothing to be ashamed of in making a profit, if the profit is a fair one and a reflection of efficiency and good work.

Marginal

There is no point in a businessman expanding his company unless the expansion will prove profitable. To investigate this more closely it is possible to compare the *marginal profit* with *marginal capital employed.* Thus when new capital is raised or profits are left in the business, it is possible to compare the increase in profit attributable to these assets.

Exercise

Thus, in the previous example, if a dividend of 10 per cent is declared taking $1,000, then $3,000 will be reinvested in the company. Now if the next years profit is $4,400 let us calculate:

1. Ratio Net Profit/Capital Invested?
2. Ratio Net Profit/Capital Employed?
3. Ratio Marginal Profit/Marginal Capital Employed?

Answers

1. $\dfrac{(4,400)}{(10,000)} \times 100 = 44$ per cent

2. $\dfrac{(4,400)}{(28,000)} \times 100 = 15.7$ per cent

3. $\dfrac{(400)}{(3,000)} \times 100 = 13.3$ per cent

We see that 1. shows an increase in profitability from 40 to 44 per cent, but this gives a slightly over-optimistic indication of continued progress. As 2. indicates there has in fact been a slight reduction in return on capital employed.

3. shows even more clearly the danger signal. Expansion is being bought at the expense of a reduction in profitability. The directors must investigate the reason for this before they proceed to draw up their plans for the coming year.

Chapter Ten
Practical Exercises

A practical exercise in the preparation of final accounts from basic information in the form of data sheets.

Learning by doing

The title of this book is *Accountancy and Book-keeping.* It would be too much to hope that reading one book would turn anyone into an expert, but it should not be unreasonable to suggest that the reader is now in a better position to understand accounting procedures. But over-academic learning is not so much use to a practical builder as work on the job. So 'learning by doing' is just as helpful to a would-be construction manager as it is to a carpenter or mason.

Practical accounting exercise

Thus the author hopes that the reader will try out his accountancy knowledge in practice as this is the best way to gain confidence and experience. To start him off, this last chapter consists of a practical accountancy exercise in which the reader can produce a balance sheet and profit and loss account for a small building business.

Data sheets

The basic information which is needed is given on the data sheets on the next five pages. These data sheets are numbered from 1 to 20 in the top right hand corner of each sheet.

First eight sheets

The first eight sheets cover receipts on the eight contracts completed in the first year of trading. You will see that some of the contracts are complete and others are still in progress. Where contracts have been finished figures appear for payments received and banked and for debtors (accounts rendered but payment from client still awaited). The total of these two figures is the value of work done on each contract.

171

①

JOB A - Receipts
(COMPLETE)

Payment received   £180

(Nothing owing)

②

JOB B - Receipts
(COMPLETE)

Payment received   £150
Invoiced but not
yet paid (Debtor)   50
                              £200

③

JOB C - Receipts
(COMPLETE)

Payment received   £460
Invoiced but not
yet paid (Debtor)   25
Value of work done   £485

④

JOB D - Receipts
(COMPLETE)

Payment received   £320

(Nothing owing)

⑤

JOB E - Receipts

Payment received	₡100
Invoiced but not yet paid (Debtor)	120
Work in progress	165
Value of work done	₡385

⑥

JOB F - Receipts

Payment received	₡600
Invoiced but not yet paid (Debtor)	500
Work in progress	320
Value of work done	₡1420

⑦

JOB G - Receipts

Invoiced but not yet paid (Debtor)	₡400
Work in progress	80
Value of work done	₡480

⑧

JOB H - Receipts

Payment received	₡300
Work in progress	50
Value of work done	₡350

JOB A ⑨

Direct Costs

Wages	$50
Materials	90
Plant & Transport	30
Sub Contractors	20
Sundries	10
TOTAL COST	$200

JOB B ⑩

Direct Costs

Wages	$60
Materials	80
Plant & Transport	20
Sundries	10
TOTAL COST	$170

JOB C ⑪

Direct Costs

Wages	$150
Materials	120
Plant & Transport	60
Sub Contractors	40
Sundries	25
TOTAL COST	$395

JOB D ⑫

Wages	$45
Material	50
Plant & Transport	35
Sundries	10
TOTAL COST	$140

(13)

JOB E

Direct Costs

Wages	₡100
Materials	85
Plant & Transport	45
Sundries	15
TOTAL COST	₡245

(14)

JOB F

Direct Costs

Wages	₡210
Materials	450
Plant & Transport	205
Sub Contractors	110
Sundries	25
TOTAL COST	₡1000

(15)

JOB G

Direct Costs

Wages	₡105
Materials	110
Plant & Transport	25
Sundries	10
TOTAL COST	₡250

(16)

JOB H

Direct Costs

Wages	₡65
Materials	70
Plant & Transport	55
Sundries	5
TOTAL COST	₡195

(17)

FIXED ASSETS

	COST ∅	LIFE (Years)
Office equipment	80	5
Plant and tools	660	6
Motor vehicles	420	4

(18)

INITIAL INVESTMENT

	∅
Owners capital	1000
10% Loan capital	1000
	2000

NOTE
Agreed fee to working
director ∅500 p.a.

(19)

CENTRAL OFFICE COSTS

Rent	∅104
Postage & telephone	35
Printing & stationery	30
Travelling expenses	40
Audit & accountancy	15
Wages -Clerk/typist	104
	∅328

(20)

CREDITORS

Materials supplier A	∅220
Materials supplier B	355
Printing bill	18
Plant hire firm	12
Petrol and oil	30
Audit & accountancy	15
	∅650

Ignore retentions

We are ignoring retentions (if any) as many contractors prefer not to take credit for these until the retention period is over and the architect has approved the release of the retention money. Thus the retention money will be left to cover any maintenance work that is asked for and the next year's profit will not be artificially reduced by additional charges on old contracts.

Work in progress

Where contracts are still in progress, an estimate is given of the value of "work in progress". This will include the value of materials on site and work done since the last valuation.

Second eight sheets

The second eight sheets (9 to 16) show the direct costs allocated to each job. These have been separated into wages for skilled and unskilled labour, materials, plant and vehicle running expenses, sub-contractors and sundries (miscellaneous items). The contractor has very sensibly allocated these costs to individual jobs so that he can check which work is most profitable and compare them with the expected costs shown in his estimate.

We will have to summarise these cost figures on a separate sheet of paper in order to build up a profit and loss account.

Fixed assets

We will need a cost figure for all the fixed assets purchased by the firm. These are shown on data sheet 17 together with the anticipated life for depreciation calculations. You will note that there is no asset figure for land and buildings as the office is rented. Remember rented property belongs to the landlord so it is *his* asset not the tenant's. Office equipment covers desk, chair and filing cabinet. Plant and tools covers such items as concrete mixer, dumper, tamping machine, shovels, forks, etc. Motor vehicles probably covers a lorry or a pick-up truck. The charge for depreciation will appear as a cost in the profit and loss account and will also be shown in the balance sheet.

Initial investment

Another vital piece of information is given on sheet 18. This shows the initial investment of the owner of the firm and the loan he has managed to raise — perhaps from a relative. We will want to know the interest payable on the loan so that it can be charged as a cost in the profit and loss account. We also see that the fee agreed as payable to the working director of the business is $500 per annum.

Central office costs

We already know the site costs, but there are some costs that cannot be allocated directly to the sites. Office rent, postage and telephone, printing and stationery, travelling costs for the manager, audit and accountancy and the wages of a clerk/typist are examples of this sort of cost. Of course, for *cost accounting* purposes and *estimating* a percentage figure can be added to labour cost or overall cost to cover these items, but for the present purpose we have to know the actual sums expended under each heading and show them separately. These figures are shown on data sheet No.19.

Creditors

Finally the builder has gone through his books to calculate the balances owing to creditors at the year end. All items which were unpaid at the end of his financial year must be shown under this heading since the creditors have first call on the assets of the business. For this particular firm, the amounts owing to various creditors are shown on data sheet No.20.

Calculation sheets

So now that all the data sheets are available, it should be possible to produce a profit and loss account and balance sheet without any further information. But to make the task a little easier, some special calculation sheets have been prepared. By filling these in correctly, the reader can automatically produce a finished balance sheet.

Calculation sheet no.1

Calculation Sheet No.1, on which direct costs and work done can be summarised, is printed on the next page.

Summary of direct costs

The top section of the calculation sheet is headed 'Summary of Direct Costs'. The reader will note that there is a space under each job for wages, materials, etc. We want to know the total cost figure for each type of cost on all the jobs so that these can be shown in the profit and loss account.

Calculation 1.

SUMMARY OF DIRECT COSTS

	JOB A	JOB B	JOB C	JOB D	JOB E	JOB F	JOB G	JOB H	TOTAL DIRECT COST
WAGES									
MATERIALS									
PLANT & TRANSPORT									
SUB CONTRACTORS									
SUNDRIES									
TOTAL COST									

SUMMARY OF WORK DONE

				TOTAL
PAYMENT RECEIVED				
DEBTORS				
WORK IN PROGRESS				
VALUE OF WORK DONE				

Total direct costs

The first stage of the calculation is to fill in the spaces in the table using the information given on data sheets 1-8. For example, under Job A, wages will be $50, materials $90, plant and transport $30 and so on. Where no costs were incurred, such as sub-contractors on Job 2, the space should be left blank. When all the figures have been transferred, the total direct costs for each sub-head of expenditure can be found by adding figures horizontally.

Summary of work done

The lower section is headed 'Summary of Work Done'. The objective is to separate out the figures for payment received, debtors, work in progress and the total value of work done. The spaces can all be filled in from data sheets 9-16. Of course, some spaces (e.g. debtors and work in progress for Job A) will be left blank. The figures can then be added horizontally to produce total figures.

Check against key sheet

Before going on to the second calculation sheet, which is printed on the next page, the reader might like to check his calculations against the key sheet at the end of this chapter.

Work done

Now we can go on to the second calculation sheet and produce a profit and loss account. To start with, we know that the value of work done (from the first sheet) is $3,820.

General cost

Inside the rectangle there are a number of items under the heading 'General Costs'. These will eventually be added to give a total general cost figure opposite the arrow.

Wages

The first item is wages. You will notice that there are separate items for office wages and site wages (within the bracket). Office wages are shown on data sheet 19 (Central Office Costs) and we have just calculated site wages on calculation sheet 1. These two can be filled in and added to give a total wages figure.

Materials, etc.

The next four items have all been calculated on the first sheet and can be transferred directly.

Calculation 2.   PROFIT & LOSS ACCOUNT

Work done   ➡

| General costs |
| Wages (Office   & Site   ) |
| Materials |
| Plant & Transport Running Costs |
| Sub Contractors |
| Sundries |
| Depreciation of fixed assets
  (see below) |
| Rent |
| Postage & telephone |
| Printing & stationery |
| Travelling expenses |
| Audit & accountancy   ➡ |

GROSS OPERATING PROFIT

LESS Interest on $1000 10% Loan   _____

LESS Fee to working director   _____

LESS Provision for taxation (Say $50)   _____

NET PROFIT (Transfer to Profit & Loss A/C) =======

CALCULATION OF DEPRECIATION

	COST $	LIFE (Years)	ANNUAL DEPRECIATION
Office equipment			
Plant & tools			
Motor vehicles			
TOTAL			

Depreciation

Then comes a tricky item — depreciation. There is a section at the bottom of the sheet for the calculation of depreciation. Cost and 'life' figures are shown on data sheet 17 (fixed assets). You will remember that the annual depreciation figure for each item is given by dividing the initial cost by the life in years so that, when the life is over, enough will have been 'saved' to pay for a replacement. When you have calculated the total depreciation, enter it in the 'general cost box'.

Rent, etc.

The last four general cost items (rent, postage, printing, etc.) are given on data sheet 19 (Central Office Costs). When you have added all the figures in the 'general cost' box enter the total on the *right* of the arrow (outside the box).

Gross operating profit

There should now be two figures in the right hand column. Subtract the total general cost from work done to give the gross operating profit.

Net profit

You can then subtract, in turn, interest on loan (10 per cent annual interest on a loan of $1,000), fee to working director (data sheet 18) and provision for taxation (say $50) to give a net profit figure.

Check against key sheet

Before continuing with the calculation, the reader might again like to check his answers against the key sheet at the end of the chapter.

Cash at bank calculation

We can now concentrate on producing the Balance Sheet. But first we must calculate a figure for cash at bank and compare it with the bank statement to ensure that there are no errors in the books (or in our arithmetic).

Calculation sheet No.3

This can be done on calculation sheet No.3

Assume started this year

We will assume that the business only came into existence at the start of the current year, so it will have begun with no bank balance and the first transaction will have been the introduction of the owner's capital and loan capital.

Calculation 3.   CASH AT BANK CALCULATION

INCOME   £

      Owners capital

      Loan capital

                               _____

      Receipts   _____

EXPENDITURE

      Direct site costs

      Central office costs

      Loan interest

      Fee to working director   _____

      Purchase cost of
       fixed assets   _____

      LESS creditors   _____

SUMMARY

      Income

      Expenditure   _____

      CASH AT BANK   _____

Income

The calculation sheet starts with a column for summarising income, and the first two items are 'owner's capital' and 'loan capital'. The next item is 'receipts' or 'payments received' as it is described in the first calculation sheet.

Expenditure

Under 'expenditure' we must first include all amounts paid or owing to others on account of purchases, wages and services rendered to the firm. For the present purpose we do not need to divide the expenditure into sub heads as we are merely trying to calculate the figure for 'cash at bank' so that it can be checked against the bank statement.

Sub total

The individual total figures for direct costs, central office costs, loan interest and directors' fees are all available in the data sheets and completed calculation sheets. These figures should be added to give a sub total before corrections are made to allow for purchase of fixed assets and money due to creditors.

Add for fixed assets

The sub total represents expenditure on current items, but to get total expenditure it is necessary to add expenditure on fixed assets made during the year. Since the fixed assets were all purchased during this year, the total cost of fixed assets should be added to the expenditure column.

Deduct for creditors

The total so far in the expenditure column covers costs incurred rather than actual expenditure, since no deduction has been made to allow for money owing to creditors as described in data sheet No.20.

Actual amount paid out

We are interested in checking the actual amounts paid into and out of the bank account, so the sum owing to the creditors must be deducted if we are to obtain the actual amount paid out in cash and cheques during the year.

Cash at bank

Since the firm started the year with a nil balance, the end year balance is given by the surplus of income (including capital introduced) over expenditure. This figure of 'Cash at Bank' will be transferred to the balance sheet.

Check against key sheet

Once again the reader might like to check his calculations against the key sheet, at the end of the chapter, before proceeding to the next stage.

Calculation No.4

Calculation sheet No.4, which will enable the reader to prepare a simple balance sheet, is printed below:

Calculation 4.   BALANCE SHEET

```
┌─────────────────────────────────────────┐
│ Work in progress                         │
│ Debtors                                  │
│ Cash at Bank          _____   ───▶     │
└─────────────────────────────────────────┘


┌─────────────────────────────────────────┐
│ LESS  Current liabilities                │
│                                          │
│ Creditors                                │
│ Taxation              _____   ───▶ ____│
└─────────────────────────────────────────┘
```

NET CURRENT ASSETS

```
┌─────────────────────────────────────────┐
│ FIXED ASSETS                             │
│ Office Equipment                         │
│ Plant and Tools                          │
│ Motor vehicles        _____           │
│                                          │
│ Less depreciation     _____   ───▶ ____│
└─────────────────────────────────────────┘
```

LESS 10% Loan Capital   _____

        NET WORTH   _____

Represented by:-

Owners Capital
Balance on P. & L. Account   _____

        NET WORTH   _____

Vertical presentation

The reader will note that the vertical form of balance sheet presentation has been chosen on this occasion.

Three boxes

The three boxes cover subsidiary calculations for Current Assets, Current Liabilities and Fixed Assets respectively.

Current assets

The top box enables the reader to calculate the current assets, which for this firm consist of Work in Progress, Debtors and Cash at Bank. All these figures are available from previous calculation sheets. When the sub total has been obtained, it should be inserted in the main column on the *right* of the arrow.

Current liabilities

In the second box we deal with current liabilities, which consist of creditors and taxation (which we shall assume has not been paid before the year end) and the total is again inserted on the *right* of the arrow.

Net current assets

You will remember that the current liabilities must be deducted from the first total to give net current assets.

Fixed assets

The third box deals with fixed assets. We first have to show the *cost* of the various assets and then deduct depreciation to give the current valuation of fixed assets. The net figure should be inserted on the *right* of the arrow.

Net worth

Then add net current assets to fixed assets to give gross value. Finally subtract the amount of loan capital outstanding to give the *net worth* of the business to its owners.

But of course Balance Sheets *must balance.*

Allocation

We know the net worth of the business, but we must show who it belongs to. So at the bottom of the sheet we insert a figure for owner's capital and for the balance on Profit and Loss Account. If we have done our job properly, we will obtain the same figure for *net worth* as calculated above. To make quite certain, the figures can be checked against the final key sheet at the end of the book.

Key to Calc/1

SUMMARY OF DIRECT COSTS

	JOB A	JOB B	JOB C	JOB D	JOB E	JOB F	JOB G	JOB H	TOTAL DIRECT COST
WAGES	50	60	150	45	100	210	105	65	785
MATERIALS	90	80	120	50	85	450	110	70	1,055
PLANT & TRANSPORT	30	20	60	35	45	205	25	55	475
SUB CONTRACTORS	20	-	40	-	-	110	-	-	170
SUNDRIES	10	10	25	10	15	25	10	5	110
TOTAL COST	200	170	395	140	245	1000	250	195	2,595

SUMMARY OF WORK DONE

	JOB A	JOB B	JOB C	JOB D	JOB E	JOB F	JOB G	JOB H	TOTAL
PAYMENT RECEIVED	180	150	460	320	100	600	-	300	2,110
DEBTORS	-	50	25	-	120	500	400	-	1,095
WORK IN PROGRESS	-	-	-	-	165	320	80	50	615
VALUE OF WORK DONE	180	200	485	320	385	1420	480	350	3,820

<u>PROFIT & LOSS ACCOUNT</u>

Work done   �→3,820

General costs	
Wages (Office 104 & Site 785)	889
Materials	1,055
Plant & Transport Running Costs	475
Sub Contractors	170
Sundries	110
Depreciation of fixed assets (see below)	231
Rent	104
Postage & telephone	35
Printing & stationery	30
Travelling expenses	40
Audit & accountancy	15 →3,154

GROSS OPERATING PROFIT   666

<u>LESS</u>   Interest on $1000 10% Loan   100

                                                566

<u>LESS</u>   Fee to working director   500

                                                66

<u>LESS</u>   Provision for taxation (Say $50)   50

NET PROFIT (Transfer to Profit & Loss A/C)   16

<u>CALCULATION OF DEPRECIATION</u>

	COST $	LIFE (Years)	ANNUAL DEPRECIATION
Office equipment	80	5	16
Plant & tools	660	6	110
Motor vehicles	420	4	105
			231

CASH AT BANK CALCULATION

INCOME		£
	Owners capital	1000
	Loan capital	1000
		2000
	Receipts	2110
		4110

EXPENDITURE		
	Direct site costs	2595
	Central office costs	328
	Loan interest	100
	Fee to working director	500
		3523
	Purchase cost of fixed assets	1160
		4683
	LESS creditors	650
		4033

SUMMARY

Income	4110
Expenditure	4033
CASH AT BANK	77

BALANCE SHEET

Work in progress	615	
Debtors	1,095	
Cash at Bank	77	➤ 1,787

LESS Current liabilities		
Creditors	650	
Taxation	50	➤ 700

NET CURRENT ASSETS   1,087

FIXED ASSETS		
Office equipment	80	
Plant and Tools	660	
Motor vehicles	420	
	1,160	
Less depreciation	231	➤ 929
		2,016

LESS 10% Loan Capital   1,000

NET WORTH   1,016

Represented by:-

Owners Capital	1,000
Balance on P. & L. Account	16
NET WORTH	1,016

BUILDING BOOKS FROM
INTERMEDIATE TECHNOLOGY PUBLICATIONS

Accounting & Book-keeping for the Small Building Contractor
Financial Planning for the Small Building Contractor
The Small Building Contractor and the Client
by Derek Miles

These three volumes are designed to help the small building contractor improve his accounting, planning and client-relationship methods. The subjects covered include: organising the office; basic book-keeping; analysis sheets; profit and loss; planning the year's work; job programmes; cash flow; investment decisions; billing procedures; work study techniques; estimating and tendering. Practical exercises and specimen forms are included.

Accounting & Book-keeping for the Small Building Contractor 190 pages. Illustrated. ISBN 0 903031 54 X. £3.95 net.
Financial Planning for the Small Building Contractor. Approx. 188 pages. Illustrated. ISBN 0 903031 55 8. £3.95 net.
The Small Building Contractor and the Client. In Preparation.

A Manual on Building Maintenance
Vol. 1: Management; Vol. 2: Methods
by Derek Miles

These companion volumes have been produced because of a lack of suitable guidance for managers of building units. This applies to both the public and private sectors in the administration and management of building sites, and in the technical aspects of maintenance work. Owing partly to the differing systems for allocating funds between capital and revenue budgets, expensive buildings are often allowed to deteriorate. This waste of resources is particularly unfortunate because repair and maintenace work is labour intensive and costly.

Vol. 1: Management deals with efficient control procedures such as resource budgets, finance, manpower, materials, equipment and provides a rational and practical system for measuring performance.

Vol. 2: Methods examines actual maintenance problems, suggests some of the more common causes of failure and sets out methods for dealing with them. These volumes make a useful and valuable contribution to increasing the operating efficiency of building units in developing countries and in the industrialised world.

"Both volumes have been written to assist maintenance staff working in developing countries to appreciate and apply maintenance techniques . . . to their particular problems. In this, the books appear successful. In the first volume, methods of maintenance management and control are clearly set out and the book would be of great use to small maintenance departments in this country. Volume 2 . . . is clearly and simply written and illustrated and should be ideal for its intended use."
— Building Technology and Management, June 1977

"The manual will be of direct assistance to those struggling with the practical application of maintenance policies and procedures."
— Indian Concrete Journal, August 1977

Vol. 1: Management 61 pages. Illustrated. ISBN 0 903031 28 0. £1.75 net.
Vol. 2: Methods 61 pages. Illustrated. ISBN 0 903031 40 X. £1.75 net.

Manual of Building Construction
by H.K. Dancy

A practical illustrated book on the construction of small buildings using local materials, suitable for a great variety of ground and climatic conditions. New edition, including metric conversion tables.

352 pages. Illustrated. ISBN 0 903031 08 6. £2.95 net.

"A practical guide to anyone intending to produce a small house or group of buildings . . . It covers the whole range of operations from choosing the site, designing and laying out the building and each stage of construction. Means of using self-contained services for the treatment of sewage and generation of electricity are also discussed for operations in which publicly provided services are not available. Since it makes no assumptions regarding the previous training of the reader the work offers a valuable support for the novice builder."
— *Building Design* (UK)

"This manual contains a wealth of information on building from scratch."
— *Rain* (USA)

Prices are correct at the time of going to press. The net price does not include postage and packing. Please add 15% to the price of publication for surface mail and UK; 35% for airmail. Orders should be sent to Intermediate Technology Publications Ltd, 9 King Street, London WC2E 8HN, UK, or to our overseas distributors. Details of these and a complete publications list are available on request.

www.ingramcontent.com/pod-product-compliance
Lightning Source LLC
Chambersburg PA
CBHW021905020426
42334CB00013B/494